Essential Skills for
3D MODELING, RENDERING, and ANIMATION

T0076582

Essential Skills for
3D MODELING, RENDERING, and ANIMATION

Nicholas Bernhardt Zeman

CRC Press
Taylor & Francis Group
Boca Raton London New York

CRC Press is an imprint of the
Taylor & Francis Group, an **informa** business

AN A K PETERS BOOK

CRC Press
Taylor & Francis Group
6000 Broken Sound Parkway NW, Suite 300
Boca Raton, FL 33487-2742

© 2015 by Taylor & Francis Group, LLC
CRC Press is an imprint of Taylor & Francis Group, an Informa business

No claim to original U.S. Government works

Printed on acid-free paper
Version Date: 20141022

International Standard Book Number-13: 978-1-4822-2412-2 (Paperback)

This book contains information obtained from authentic and highly regarded sources. Reasonable efforts have been made to publish reliable data and information, but the author and publisher cannot assume responsibility for the validity of all materials or the consequences of their use. The authors and publishers have attempted to trace the copyright holders of all material reproduced in this publication and apologize to copyright holders if permission to publish in this form has not been obtained. If any copyright material has not been acknowledged please write and let us know so we may rectify in any future reprint.

Except as permitted under U.S. Copyright Law, no part of this book may be reprinted, reproduced, transmitted, or utilized in any form by any electronic, mechanical, or other means, now known or hereafter invented, including photocopying, microfilming, and recording, or in any information storage or retrieval system, without written permission from the publishers.

For permission to photocopy or use material electronically from this work, please access www.copyright.com (http://www.copyright.com/) or contact the Copyright Clearance Center, Inc. (CCC), 222 Rosewood Drive, Danvers, MA 01923, 978-750-8400. CCC is a not-for-profit organization that provides licenses and registration for a variety of users. For organizations that have been granted a photocopy license by the CCC, a separate system of payment has been arranged.

Trademark Notice: Product or corporate names may be trademarks or registered trademarks, and are used only for identification and explanation without intent to infringe.

Library of Congress Cataloging-in-Publication Data

Zeman, Nicholas Bernhardt.
   Essential skills for 3D modeling, rendering, and animation / author, Nicholas Bernhardt Zeman.
      pages cm
   Includes bibliographical references and index.
   ISBN 978-1-4822-2412-2 (pbk.)
   1. Computer animation. 2. Three-dimensional modeling. I. Title.

TR897.7.Z46 2014
006.6'96--dc23

2014039017

Visit the Taylor & Francis Web site at
http://www.taylorandfrancis.com

and the CRC Press Web site at
http://www.crcpress.com

Contents

Preface

Late at night, 1997, in some little one-bedroom apartment on Lexington Avenue, in Lexington, Kentucky, I installed my very first 3D software on my self-built HP Windows 95 workstation. It had 64 megabytes of RAM and an Intel Pentium 32 gigahertz processor. Caligari Truespace was an ancient VRML (Virtual Reality Markup Language) authoring software that I had downloaded for free. It was my very first experience with 3D graphics.

I had seen it in movies. I had seen it in video games. But I had never really held the tools of creation in my hands and manipulated objects in 3D space before. I eagerly navigated around the interface of the default scene file, which was strewn with various old-timey 3D objects: a teapot, a house, a spider, and a roller coaster. I selected the spider and chose the "rotate" tool, and for the very first time in my life, I manipulated a model in three dimensions on a computer screen.

There was no going back. From that one particular moment in time and space, a light went on in my head and I was obsessed. I could not stop thinking about 3D animation. The possibilities exploded. The next 14 years of my life would be a single-minded drive down that same road, without ever stopping to wonder if I was on the right path. 3D graphics were my passion and aspiration. And although that path was ultimately successful, I had a long way to go in terms of my basic understanding.

Here is the problem: I had no idea what I was doing. I didn't know a damn thing about 3D graphics. I didn't know what a vertex was, I didn't know how materials and lights worked, and I didn't know the difference between Euler and Quaternion rotations or how to edit tangents in a motion graph. I knew, essentially, bupkiss. I bought books, but they were so technical that I had no idea what they were saying. I was not a stupid person. But even a smart person cannot learn 30 years of computer graphics by reading a technical manual on VRML specifications. In 1997, there were no Art Institutes, no ITT classes, and no university courses that could make any sense of all this new stuff I was being exposed to. There was no YouTube. There was no Google. There was no resource for a guy like me.

So, I taught myself. But in doing so, I tried to create 3D animations and effects without having any idea exactly how to do it. I didn't know the basics. I just wanted to make something "cool." But when you try to make art without knowing how to paint, you don't usually do a very good job.

I began to learn things from experience—my first jobs, my first work with other 3D artists who showed me a few things. I learned how to do specific jobs on specific software, but my general understanding of how all this stuff "worked" was vague and sketchy. When you learn to use specific software to do specific things, you can do a good job, but you end up a lot like a trained monkey. You can push buttons in a sequence without really knowing what they are for. I wanted more than that.

Time went on, and my skills and understanding grew. I was working full time by then for Red Zone, a game developer for Playstation (which was eventually bought by Sony Computer Entertainment America). I learned some new things, new skills, and new specifics. We ran into problems with things, and the solutions to those problems made sense in various ways, but despite my skills and technical expertise that grew as a result of my daily involvement with games and game development, I was still lacking a fundamental understanding of the mechanics going on under the hood. I could drive the car, but I had no idea how the engine worked! A great racecar driver can succeed without ever peeking under the hood, but if the car breaks down he or she will be stranded.

The years went on, and my knowledge was constantly and exponentially increased by the daily grind and repetition of various problems that occur in modeling, rendering, and animation. I knew how to fix all kinds of problems, but I had never learned certain basic elements of 3D graphics.

Fast forward several years, after my exit from my career as a game developer and the beginning of my academic career. My master's degree was in instructional design, which I had never thought I would use again, but I was asked to create a curriculum for learning the "basics" of 3D graphics. As I started work on this curriculum, I realized that there was a lot of stuff I still didn't know! Luckily, with my 14 years of experience as a modeler, animator, and rigger, I knew enough to piece together what I didn't know. As I transitioned into the role of a professor, I began teaching these essential skills and knowledge blocks, and tweaking them as I saw how people learned and reconstructed my lessons on their own.

The result is this book, which I have thoughtfully constructed to give the complete novice and even the experienced artist a basic foundational understanding of all things that make up the core of 3D computer graphics, written for the non-technical mind. It is written to impart everything you need to know about 3D graphics, without being tied to an individual piece of software. While the examples are specifically taken from Autodesk Maya, they rarely mention anything tied to the specific software tools (the most notable exception is in the Rendering and Materials section), but instead focus on the common elements of all 3D graphics and how they work.

As you go through this book, keep in mind that this stuff isn't simple—in fact, it is extremely complex. This book is intended to distill that complexity and focus on only the essential skills and knowledge that you will need to start your path down the road to becoming a skilled 3D artist. Good luck! It is not a quick path. My best advice is to learn the basics, gather your skills in what suits you the best, and focus on that one thing.

Additional material is available from the CRC Web site: http://www.crcpress.com/product/ISBN/9781482224122.

About the Author

Nicholas Bernhardt Zeman started his career in 3D graphics at the University of Kentucky, where during graduate school he began working in 3D Studio Max for the first time. Determined to make 3D graphics and games his career path, he left Kentucky for San Diego, where he was offered a job at Red Zone Interactive, a then-small company making the NFL Gameday series for Sony Computer Entertainment. He continued working for them as an expert in character rigging, facial rigging, and facial animation after they were purchased by SCEA until the team was disbanded and the NFL Gameday series was cancelled after losing rights to EA for the football franchise. After that, he worked briefly as an animator and facial rigger for SCEA's motion capture and cinematic studio, working on SOCOM 3, among other titles. He was quickly hired by Take Two Interactive in San Rafael, where he continued to develop and manage character rigs on the NBA 2K series, All-Pro Football 2K8, MLB 2K9-10, and NHL 2K9. After almost 12 years in character rigging for sports games, he decided to leave the employment of game developers and focus on the academic pursuit of interactive development as a Professor at Northern Kentucky University in the Media Informatics Department and begin his own digital media technology company, RHZ Development LLC, where he continues to consult and produce functional games through gamification, mobile apps, and mobile games under the studio brand "Little Fish Games" and RHZ Development.

Introduction

WHAT IS 3D ART? HOW DOES IT WORK?

3D computer-generated art is a complex thing. We see it all the time in games, in movies, and on TV, but to the aspiring 3D artist or game developer, the entirety of it can be a little daunting. In order to start understanding the individual elements of 3D, you have to understand the big picture. 3D art is divided into three separate elements: modeling (geometry), rendering, and animation.

Modeling and geometry are the description of objects and the space they occupy. To understand this part requires some aspects of sculpting, or knowing how a surface or object flows in 3D space. First, you must understand the basic tenets of the space within which your objects and geometry exist, and then you must learn the tools with which to build and edit those objects and geometry. Modeling is the first step in the field because without geometry and objects there is nothing to render or animate.

Key elements of 3D modeling that you will learn in this book:

1. 3D space, the grid, and coordinate systems

2. Polygon modeling

3. Polygonal modeling tools and techniques

4. Non-uniform rational b-splines (NURBS) curves and curve-based modeling

5. NURBS modeling techniques

6. Tesselation and adaptive geometry

RENDERING, LIGHTING, AND MATERIALS

Rendering is the second part of this textbook. Rendering is essentially converting the geometry into pixels on a screen, which requires lights and materials. Setting up lights and materials is done for the primary purpose of turning your geometry into pixels on the screen, which will then appear to be an object. Materials and lighting can go very deep, but never forget that your intended objective is to set up the geometry to be seen, whether in real-time for a game or in a series of images for a video or film. Without lighting or rendering, you would not be able to see the geometry at all (although it would still technically be there).

Key elements of rendering you will learn in this book are as follows:

1. Normals and the essence of shading

2. 3D lights and light properties

3. Cameras and camera properties

4. Materials and shaders

5. Texture maps

6. UV mapping techniques

7. Real time vs. software rendering

ANIMATION

Animation adds the fourth dimension to your 3D art: time. The values of things change over time, and the animator controls those changes by setting keyframes at certain places. The software figures out the places in between the saved keyframes, and plays the animation by rendering a frame for every frame of the animation, which is then played at a certain rate. It is no different from old-school hand-drawn animation; it just uses the computer to do all the grunt work for you.

Key elements of animation you will learn in this book are as follows:

1. Keyframing and interpolation

2. Hand-animation and key poses

3. Graph editing and motion curves

4. Acceleration and deceleration

Using this book, you will not become a fabulous modeler, material editor, or animator. Rather, this book is designed to teach you how all these things work together to form the basis of 3D computer art. The fundamentals are often overlooked by those entering the field, if for no other reason than a lack of content that clearly and definitively states them in a conceptual manner. I wish I had had a guideline to foundational concepts when I had started, so I am writing this to make it easier for the beginner or even the experienced artist to continue his or her pursuit of excellence in games, video, or design.

CHAPTER 1

Understanding 3D Space

HOW DO WE KNOW WHERE THINGS ARE IN 3D GRAPHICS?

Cartesian Mapping and 3D Coordinates

If I asked you, "Where is the Earth?" what would you say?

You might say, "In relation to what?" The sun? Mars? Anywhere? Nowhere? This might start to sound like an exercise in philosophy, but the point I am trying to make is that location is *relative*. We know where things *are* because we can measure them against various reference points (which can be as simple as our own position).

In the real world, we don't have any finite points in space where we can measure things from—we simply create a relative idea of position by measuring it from another point. Imagine, for instance, we had a duplicate of ourselves somewhere on Mars. Let us also assume that Earth and Mars were not moving at all. How would we know where our doppelganger was, relative to where we were? We could stretch an imaginary tape measure between us, and then we could get an exact distance. We can measure all things from our precise position and get an idea of where the Martian version of us is, relative to where we are, as shown in Figure 1.1.

HOW DO WE DETERMINE THESE POSITIONS?

The Grid

Much like this method of locating things, the world of 3D graphics depends on a giant "grid" or location coordinate system, to exist. The 3D grid is an extension of our method of measuring distance; essentially, it is

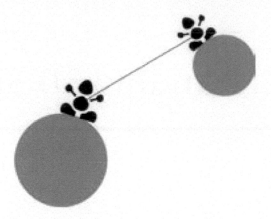

FIGURE 1.1 You and your Martian clone with a line drawn between you—it is easy to calculate distance when you are not in motion!

a giant graph that encompasses the entirety of the 3D world. This grid is known as Cartesian mapping.

The grid is separated into three dimensions: x, y, and z. These three dimensions are responsible for locating everything that ever goes into 3D graphics. You see, in a 3D world you have a single point in space from which all other things are measured. This point in space is called the **world origin**. In Figure 1.2, you can see the world origin where the lines in bold intersect. Everything in 3D space is located from this point, which never changes. This is called the **global coordinate system**.

When working with 3D graphics, there are two types of coordinate systems: Y-up and Z-up. Y-up is generally the standard for animation, and Z-up is generally the standard for architecture and engineering. Why? Let's look at the 2D grid system and see why.

A 2D grid is always flat. The X-axis is horizontal, and the Y-axis is vertical. Pretty simple, right? Let's make it more complex by adding the third dimension, Z. Now, if you are an animator you see the grid as a screen, facing toward your field of vision. In this case, to your right is the positive X, to your left is the negative X. Straight up is the positive Y, and straight down is the negative Y. Where is the Z? The Z is away from you or towards you. Therefore, as objects move away from you on the screen they are moving in the negative Z-axis. The arrows in Figure 1.3 are color-coded, where X is red, Y is green, and Z is blue.

FIGURE 1.2   The Cartesian mapping system allows us to map coordinates in 3D space by choosing a single point from which all other locations are measured.

FIGURE 1.3   A manipulator handle in Maya. Most 3D software uses this color-coding and appearance to give you the ability to move objects around in 3D space using a mouse. The arrows constrain the movement to one axis.

If you are an architect and you are laying out a plan for the design of a building, chances are that you are using a blueprint. When you are looking at a blueprint, the positive X-axis is to your right and the negative is to your left. The positive Y-axis is *toward you*, and the negative Y-axis is *away from you*. The positive Z-axis is up, and the negative is down. This is different from the animator's view because you are looking down on the blueprint and making it 3D would extrude the building towards you.

For the sake of this book, we will always be working in the Y-up world. However, you should always be aware of the Z-up world and how to deal with information from it.

WHAT ARE THE COORDINATE SYSTEMS? ARE THERE MORE THAN JUST ONE?

Global and Local Coordinate Systems

OK, so now that we start to understand the setup of this coordinate system, let's look at how the grid operates. The grid is an infinite set of coordinates that determines where a **transform** is. A transform is simply a point in space. That point in space can be moved, and anything that is connected to that transform will move with it. A transform has no volume, and it takes up no space. It is simply a way of determining where an object is in space. If we create an object in any 3D software, it will create a transform for us that is associated with that object. That transform will then be measured from the world origin in global space. Therefore, the transform will be given three sets of coordinates, corresponding to the three axes in the following order: x, y, z. It is written in code form as (x, y, z). So we can say our transform here has a global space value of (0, 0, 0), shown in Figures 1.4 and 1.5.

If we move this object, the world space coordinates will reflect this movement. You can see that I have moved the object three units in the X-axis and now the global coordinates are (3, 0, 0). If I move it around in the other two dimensions, it will be located at (4, 1, 5). You can see that no matter where I put this object in the world, it will be located by its transform, which is a single point in space and will *always* have coordinates based on the world origin. This is how the computer calculates everything in 3D graphics; without this transform and world origin, movement and position could not be determined! (See Figures 1.6 and 1.7.)

FIGURE 1.4   Transforms with the translate, rotate, and scale listed in numerical value. They are always read in values of (x,y,z).

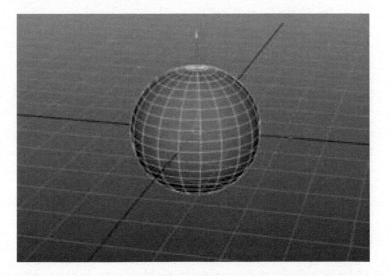

FIGURE 1.5   A polygon sphere on the grid.

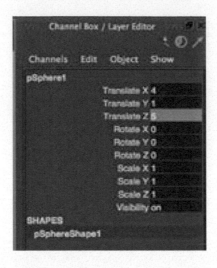

FIGURE 1.6   Numerical values entered into the transforms of pSphere1.

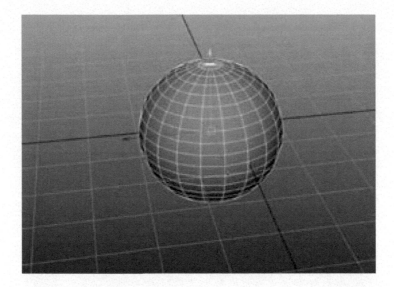

FIGURE 1.7   Manually transforming the object with a mouse; in Maya, this method uses what is called a *manipulator*.

WHAT IS LOCAL SPACE?

Hierarchies and Local Transforms

The global (or world) coordinate system is not the only way to locate an object. There are **relative** locations for every point in space, especially if they are attached to another object. We call this the **local coordinate system**, which determines where an object is in relation to another object to which it is attached. You can think of this as we are "attached" to Earth. If you are living on Earth, then you are definitely attached to Earth and your position is changing every second, relative to some point off Earth (let's say the Sun). Because you cannot be separated from Earth (and if you did it would be very unfortunate for you), we consider you to be a "child" of Earth, and Earth is called your **parent**. In this relationship, known as a **hierarchy**, you inherit all the movements of the parent object. Your position, relative to Earth, is your **local position** because it is measured from your parent object. Therefore, you might be standing still, which means that you aren't moving relative to your parent, but your global position (measured from some other stable position like the Sun) would be in a constant state of flux because Earth is rotating around its own axis and around the Sun as well.

Just like this relationship between you and Earth, the relationship between a transform of an object and the pieces that make up that object is both global and local. An object in 3D graphics consists of sub-objects, which construct it in some way (we will explore this later); the sub-object points that construct it have positions that are relative to the object transform *and* to the world origin.

Hierarchies and coordinate systems may seem complex, and in fact, they can get quite difficult to understand. However, the basic notion of one object being connected to another should be quite familiar to us. For instance, look at your hand. Your hand can move around the space in your body while your body stands still. We can say then that your hand is moving in local space. However, if you start walking around and waving your hand, your hand is moving both in relationship to your body, and moving *with* your body. It is permanently connected. Therefore, the wave is the wave no matter where you do it, but your body is moving in global space (and, hence, so is your hand). This idea of hierarchies should be natural to us because this is how our own skeletal system works.

HOW DO I CHANGE AN OBJECT'S POSITION IN SPACE?

Transforms

There are three basic ways we can transform an object: translate, rotate, and scale. These are considered the basic transforms. Each transform type has a pivot, or place from where the transform is calculated. Generally, the transform pivots are all in the same location, but some programs allow you to put each transform in different places. This **pivot** is essentially the transform node, as discussed before. What is really changing in any 3D object is the **components** of which that object consist, while keeping their relative positions from one another. The transform node is just a way of making them translate, rotate, or scale from a single point in space. In Figure 1.8, you can see that the points which make up this cube are in a different place than the pivot, which is indicated by the yellow box with the arrows sticking out (in Maya this is called a **manipulator**). All of the points of the cube in Figure 1.8 will move with this pivot when the transform object is moved. If the cube is rotated, the points making up the cube will be rotated around this point in space while keeping their relative positions to one another—that is, the cube will still be a cube, but it will rotate around the transform pivot point. The same goes for the scale. The points in space will scale inward or outward from the pivot point.

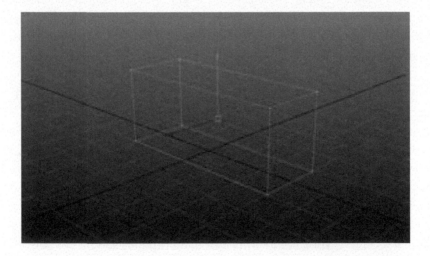

FIGURE 1.8   The points that make up the object, called *vertices*, inherit the transforms from the transform node, which transforms them in space relative to the *pivot point*, as indicated by the position of the manipulator handle.

Translation is the simplest transform. It is just moving an object in space. All of the sub-objects of the transform move along, keeping their relative distances from one another (which are their local coordinates). You can translate any object on the X-, Y-, or Z-axes. These are separated into three channels that can be edited independently. You can translate an object on the global or the local coordinate system. It will be the same as long as these two are aligned. This gets more complicated as we start to rotate the object.

Rotation is an interesting transform. Rotating an object is really just translating it, but around a specific point in space. Therefore, wherever your pivot is, the object will translate itself in orbit, around that pivot. Imagine a ball on a string. If you spin the ball on that string, it will be moving in space. However, it will be moving around the point at which you are spinning it, in a perfect circle. This is how rotation works—it spins the object around a point in space. This happens like a nail with a string in it; if you hold on to the string and walk, you will always form a perfect circle around the point where the nail is set. This nail represents the **pivot** point of the object. In Figure 1.9, you can see how the points of the cube revolve around the pivot point but maintain their respective distances from each other perfectly. This is an example of a hierarchy. The points inherit the movement of the transform.

Rotation happens in degrees—0 for the initial point and 360 for the point at which it has rotated once, but is in that same position. There are

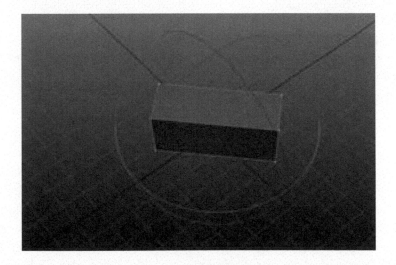

FIGURE 1.9   A cube showing the planes of rotation.

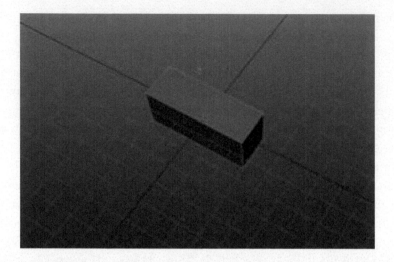

FIGURE 1.10 The world and the object are lined up.

two types of rotation calculations in 3D graphics: Euler and Quaternion. Euler (pronounced "oiler") separates the rotation into three channels: x, y, and z. Quaternion is a different system, but we are going to be working strictly in Euler for the sake of this book (and Euler is the more common system for animation). That means we have three channels in which to rotate an object (x, y, and z).

Now here is the complicated thing—and why we need to have a good understanding of global vs. local coordinates. When you rotate an object 45 degrees in the Y-axis, the orientation changes. Notice how in Figures 1.10 and 1.11 the arrows are pointing in different directions? What has happened is that the orientation of the cube has changed in its object or local space (sometimes the two terms can mean different things) and is no longer aligned with the world axis.

This means that the cube can now be translated in one of two coordinate systems—see how the translate X is different between global and local? If you translate X in the global coordinate system, it moves along the world X-axis. However, if you move it in the local coordinate system, which is unique to the cube, it will move it on a diagonal! This is because the orientation of the pivot has changed and the cube's X-axis no longer matches up with the world X-axis. When you transform an object, you always have a choice about which coordinate system you are transforming it on. All software programs allow you at least to choose between the global and the local coordinate system. Some, like Maya, also allow you to

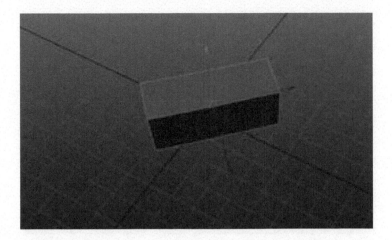

FIGURE 1.11 Our object is no longer aligned with the world—its object transforms are now different so if you move it along the Object X axis, it will not move along the World X axis.

move the object based on its parent axis (which Maya calls "local") and its local axis (which Maya calls "object" space).

Scale is a transform that changes the relative spacing between subobjects, but increases the space between components. Like the real world, it changes how "big" something is, or how much "space" is between the components that make up that space. Scale can occur on the local or global coordinate system, and scale can occur in a non-uniform manner; that is, you can scale independently on the X-, Y-, or Z-axis, both locally and globally. The default or "zero" value for scale is 1. Changing scale values to less than 1 makes it smaller, and larger than 1 makes it bigger. This refers to percentage, and a value of 1 equals 100%. If you scale an object to 0, it will essentially disappear because all of the components that it consists of will be scrunched into a single point in space (which will correspond to the pivot point of the x form.)

FROM WHERE DOES AN OBJECT MOVE WHEN YOU MOVE IT?

Pivots and Snaps

Because we now know that pivots are the point in space from which the geometry is calculated, we can now look at **pivot mode**, or the act of changing the pivot point of an object while leaving the object in the same spot. We change the position of the pivot relative to the object in order to adjust

FIGURE 1.12   The pivot point of a cube moved to the corner point. Now everything will transform relative to that point.

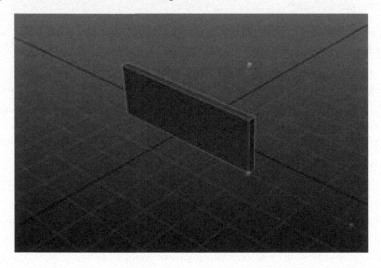

FIGURE 1.13   The result of scaling from the altered pivot point is drastically different from scaling from the center.

from which point the transformations occur. In most 3D programs, there is a pivot mode or other manner in which to transform the pivot while leaving the object alone. As you can see in Figures 1.12 and 1.13, I have moved the pivot of our cube to the lower point of the cube (using the point snap as detailed next). Now when I make any transform, such as a scale, you can clearly see that the action has happened from a different location than the center of the object where the pivot was originally located.

Snaps are a way of aligning specific points to other specific points. The most commonly used snaps in 3D are Grid, Point/Vertex, and Curve (although we will explore Curve Snaps later in the book). A snap is simply a method to ensure a single point in space, like a Transform Node, is placed exactly onto another point in space, such as a grid point or a vertex (part of geometry). They are there to allow the 3D developer to know exactly where objects exist and are transformed from, especially when aligning them to one another. Without snaps, it would be very difficult for the modeler or developer to ensure that things are exactly where they need to be in relation to other things. "Eyeballing" is a term commonly used in 3D art to refer to the act of lining up two or more objects in a scene by using the unconstrained move tool and your eye to determine their proximity. Eyeballing is really a bad way of doing this because it takes longer to get right and ultimately lacks a lot of precision. Precision is something important in *all* 3D, regardless of whether you are working in games, film, or engineering. We all want to be creative, but the trick is to organize your scenes and 3D objects in such a way as to facilitate that creativity. If you do not align things and snap things, your scene is likely to be a mess and cause problems down the road with rendering and other calculations. An experienced 3D artist relies heavily on snapping and precise transforms for this reason.

CAN I RESET THE TRANSFORMS AFTER MOVING MY OBJECT?

Freezing and Re-Setting Transforms

In many 3D programs, there is an ability to change the local transforms of the object to a value of zero, without changing the position of the object. This is often referred to as "freezing" or "re-setting" the transforms. This creates an under-the-hood offset for the transforms, which allows the animator to animate from a value of 0 instead of something weird like 102.44. If you are animating an object's translate X, you would much rather use 0 as your starting value than 102.44. It makes more sense and it is much easier to calculate in your head. However, if your object was positioned somewhere in your scene properly and the translate X value is something arbitrary like 102.44, you can "freeze" the transforms, which will report a local value of 0 in the translate X channel. The global position of the object will be the same because it is always absolute; however, the local position will report 0.0 and allow you to offset values from that value from that point on. Sometimes, however, when moving data back and forth from program to program (especially to and from game engines) these internal offsets are disregarded and your object will appear to be in a different place. This is when you must re-set the transforms.

"Re-setting" transforms of a 3D object puts the pivot point back at the world origin and removes all offset values, without moving the object. This option is to remove all those internal offsets that have possibly been created when working with the object in space. It is very important to be able to perform this because often many programs will not accept these internal offsets, and characters you have created and animated will not come in the appropriate places from software to software. This is especially important in modern workflows where you may use one program to model, one to rig, one to animate, one to do motion capture, and one to develop your game. You must have the basic transform structure of your models and objects set properly in order to be consistent among them all. Because of this issue, most major software programs have built-in tools to adjust your local transforms without changing the actual position of the objects you have created.

EXERCISE: TRANSFORMING OBJECTS IN SPACE WITH MAYA

This video-based tutorial will illustrate how to move objects in basic 3D space, and how all of the transforms are calculated using Maya 2014. I do not have specific instructions on how to use Maya itself (which would take its own book!) but more specific step-by-step instructions on how to do the specific task in Maya. I highly suggest going through the introductory 5-minute training videos that come with Maya, just to learn how to navigate through 3D space and easily perform the selections, transforms, and operations that I will be going through. Using Maya is very much like driving a stick-shift car; it requires one hand on the keyboard and one hand on a 3-button mouse in order to use it properly. There are hundreds of keyboard shortcuts and commands, which I will instruct you to use as we go through the exercises. These exercises are meant to be used in conjunction with the training videos on the website, which you will follow along with the step-by-step instructions in this book. The keyboard shortcuts and mouse controls will be illustrated on the screen as the videos play to make it easier for you to catch what is happening with the controls. The images and videos are taken from the Mac OSX version of the software, which looks slightly different from the Windows version, but should be close enough for you to follow along. There really is not much discernible difference in the Windows and

FIGURE 1.14　The polygons sub-module.

Mac interface, but there are a few keyboard commands that differ due to the Mac proprietary keyboard. Note that all keyboard shortcuts described are using lowercase letters unless specifically stated otherwise, in which case it would be denoted as "shift + w," and not "W."

Step 1

Make sure that you are in the "polygons" module of Maya, which you can choose on the upper left-hand corner of the menu (see Figure 1.14).

Step 2

Go to the "Create" menu, which will be a pull-down menu on the top panel of the software. Choose Create > Polygon Primitives > Cube. This will allow you to drag a cube on the grid in the perspective view. Your first click and drag will control the depth and width of the cube, after which the release of the mouse and subsequent click will control the height of the cube. On the left-hand side of the screen, you will see the Tool Box, or where the tools to select and transform your object are (Figure 1.17). On the right-hand side of the screen you will see the Channel Box, which is where all of the transforms are listed numerically and can be edited that way (Figure 1.18). The transform values you see here will reflect *local* values, which are derived from the parent of the object. If the object is a parent of the world, which means it has no parent, then these values will reflect the world space coordinates as measured from the world origin.

In order to switch between shaded 3D mode and wireframe 3D mode, use the hotkeys "4" and "5," respectively.

The keyboard shortcuts to select, translate, rotate, and scale your objects are "q," "w," "e," and "r," respectively.

Create	Display	Window	Assets	Select	Mesh	Edit Mesh

NURBS Primitives ►
Polygon Primitives ►
Volume Primitives ►
Lights ►
Cameras ►

CV Curve Tool
EP Curve Tool ☐
Bezier Curve Tool ☐
Pencil Curve Tool ☐
Arc Tools ►

Measure Tools ►

Scene Assembly ►

Text ☐
Adobe(R) Illustrator(R) Object... ☐

Construction Plane ☐
Free Image Plane ☐
Locator
Annotation...

Empty Group
Sets ►

Sphere ☐
Cube ☐
Cylinder ☐
Cone ☐
Plane ☐
Torus ☐
Prism ☐
Pyramid ☐
Pipe ☐
Helix ☐
Soccer Ball ☐
Platonic Solids ☐

✔ Interactive Creation
✔ Exit On Completion

FIGURE 1.15   The Create Polygon Primitive Menu.

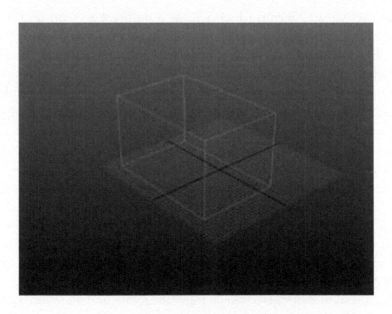

FIGURE 1.16   The cube as created by dragging the window.

FIGURE 1.17 The Tool Box where you can select, translate, rotate, or scale objects.

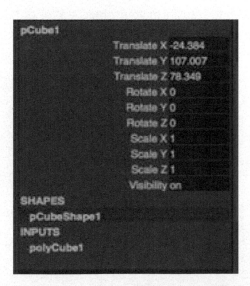

FIGURE 1.18 The Channel Box has the transforms available for type-in value changes. It also contains the construction history of an object, which has all of the operations that are "stacked" or put in order to create the final output of an object.

Step 3: Type-in Transforms

Experiment by typing transform values into the translate, rotate, and scale values in the Channel Box. Note how it affects the object.

Step 4: The Pivot, the Manipulator, and Transforming in 3D Space

The pivot of an object is the point in space from which the transforms of the object are measured. This is your very first important lesson in 3D space and coordinates—that point is not only vital to how the object transforms, but also it is transformable itself! Notice that when you choose the Move Tool and select your cube by dragging over the object, a colored-crosshair with arrows on the ends will appear at the center (Figure 1.19). This is called a manipulator. You can translate, rotate, and scale an object in 3D space with the manipulator. The translate manipulator looks like Figure 1.19, with arrows coming out of the crosshair and those arrows allow you to constrain the object to one dimension at a time, for greater accuracy when manipulating the object in 3D space. The rotation and scale manipulator are shown in Figures 1.20 and 1.21, respectively, and they all use the color-coding of red = X-axis, green = Y-axis, and blue = Z-axis. Use these manipulators to practice translating, rotating, and scaling your object in 3D space. In the Tool Settings, you can choose which coordinate space on which to transform your object—World, Local, Object, and Normal (and some other custom options). World is global space, which is measured against the world origin when translating, or against the world

FIGURE 1.19   The translate manipulator.

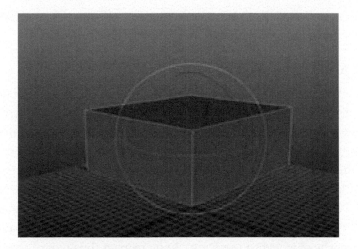

FIGURE 1.20   The rotate manipulator.

FIGURE 1.21   The scale manipulator.

direction axis when rotating or scaling. Local is based on the coordinates of the object's parent, which is important to keep in mind, but also all exercises in this book will assume that the objects are not parented to anything else, which means they are parented to the world, which also means that their local coordinates and the world coordinate space are identical. *Object* space changes with the object, and is easy to understand if you rotate your object in local space and then try to translate it in object space it will move along its own axis instead of the world.

In order to "snap" the object to grid points, hold down the "x" key while using the translate manipulator.

Step 5: Adjusting the Pivot

OK, now that we know how to move objects around and manipulate them in Maya, we can learn how to change the position of that pivot. Why would you want to do this? Well, because the object is manipulated *from* that point in space, changing its location will vastly alter how your transforms affect it. It will also give you the ability to create a point of reference from which you can "snap" your object to other positions in space or other objects. Using the "insert" key on a PC, or the "fn – left arrow" key combo on a Mac, you will enter pivot mode. Pivot mode switches your ability to transform the object with the ability to transform the pivot of that object. When you are in pivot mode, you can move the pivot anywhere you like. We are going to snap the pivot, using the Point Snap Tool, to the cube's lower-right corner (by holding down the "v" key while moving it). Once you have "snapped" the pivot to the intended point, you can exit pivot mode and see the changes when you transform it, most especially rotating and scaling the object.

Holding the "v" key down engages your point snap.

On a Mac, "fn left arrow" or "insert" on a PC enters pivot mode.

Step 6: Building a Staircase

Now that we have all that, we are going to build a simple staircase with the tools we have learned how to use. Scale and position your box on the grid as it looks in Figure 1.22, with the pivot point at the rear corner. Make sure the box is snapped to the grid securely by using your grid snap option.

Now you will duplicate this big, flat cube by going to the Edit > Duplicate pull-down menu, or using the "control – d" keyboard shortcut. This will duplicate the object exactly on top of the current object. Once you have duplicated the object, move it using the point snap option ("v" key) and snap it to the box below it. Now you can scale your second cube, constrained in the Z-axis, and see how it will change the size in only one direction, which will make a two-stair staircase, as you can see in Figure 1.23.

Now repeat this process, as many times as you like, making sure that the snaps are on when you translate the next box, and scale it only in the Z-axis to change the depth of the stair piece. Eventually you will have a perfectly aligned staircase, like Figure 1.24.

FIGURE 1.22   Snap the pivot to the lower corner.

FIGURE 1.23   Now duplicate the object and snap it to the one below it using the point snap. The two will be perfectly aligned, based on the corner point.

FIGURE 1.24   Continue to duplicate and snap, scaling the cubes in the Z-axis as you go. You will have created a simple staircase.

Conclusion

In this exercise, you have learned the following skills using Maya:

- How to create primitive polygonal objects

- How to use the Channel Box or 3D manipulators to translate, rotate, and scale objects in 3D space

- How to snap to the grid and to points

- How to adjust the location of an object's pivot

- How to duplicate objects

- How to snap objects to other objects

CHAPTER 2

Polygonal Geometry

WHAT IS A MODEL?

Basic Polygon Concepts

In order to answer that question, we are going to have to get down and dirty with something most of us creative types loathe: mathematics. But don't worry; math is not so hard when the computer gives you all the correct answers. A computer, after all, is simply a giant, fancy calculator with a bunch of graphics working on top of it. All it can really do is calculate equations. The good news is that we do not have to do that hard math work. However, we do need to know how to tell it to work for us. It is like driving a car. You don't need to know the chemistry behind a combustion engine, but you do need to know which pedal is the gas and which one is the brake (or else your morning commute is going to be really interesting!).

A model is anything in your 3D software package that is constructed of **geometry.** Remember geometry in high school? Wasn't that fun? If you are a creative type, like me, I doubt that it was very much fun at all. Geometry is an offshoot of math that deals with shapes. Moreover, shapes are what rule the world of modeling, from the most detailed Pixar characters to the most basic of iPhone games. The one, single important shape that is the building block for all others, the "atom" of the 3D geometrical world, is the triangle (Figure 2.2).

A triangle is just what is seems. It is a shape with three sides. In 3D graphic-speak we call this a **polygon.** A polygon is any multisided object that consists of triangles, which is the basic building block of all 3D shapes. Here are the **components** of the polygon:

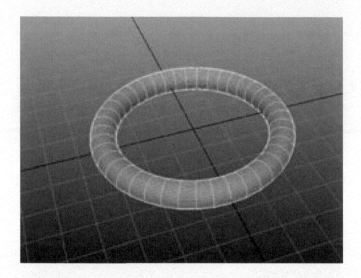

FIGURE 2.1   A polygon torus or donut shape.

FIGURE 2.2   A polygon triangle.

1. **Vertex:** The most important aspect of a polygon, the vertex is a point in space that has coordinates. These points in space are connected and create the objects you see.

2. **Edge:** An edge connects two vertices together.

3. **Face:** The face is all of the space in between the connected vertices. This is what is turned into pixels and displayed on your screen.

4. **Normal:** The normal is the perpendicular, or 90-degree angle to the face. The normal is a derived value, or something that changes because of the positions of the other sub-objects. It cannot be transformed by itself.

So, those are the pieces that make up our friend, the triangle. The polygon could not exist without all three of them. We can transform them each using translate, rotate, and scale. Only the vertex, however, will move independently; the rest are dependent upon their connected vertices. This is why a good modeler, or digital sculptor, will mostly do transformations at the vertex level. It is far more dependable. There are exceptions, of course, but generally the modeler sees the object in terms of *points*, even when there are thousands of them. This is because everything about a model is dependent on these points. The **vertices** exist independently of one another. All of the other sub-objects, edges, faces, and normals, are completely dependent on a vertex to exist. An edge requires two vertices, and a face requires at least three vertices. A vertex, however, requires nothing but itself. A model consists of those points, strung together by edges, which form faces, which are defined by the space in between the edges.

BUT HOW CAN TRIANGLES BUILD SMOOTH SURFACES?

Triangulation and Polygons

Now, everything you see that has been created in 3D at one point is broken down into triangles (yes, even *Toy Story 3* and *Shrek*). The reason for this is that the computer does not understand anything else in terms of 3D graphics. In order for any object to be displayed on your screen, it must be broken down into the simplest element possible, which is a triangle. Even when you have **quads**, which are four-sided polygons, they are being broken down into triangles for you (you just don't see it happening). Take the sphere in Figure 2.3, for example. It has six sides, each side having four faces. If you notice, however, when I turn on "show triangles" you can see that the computer is secretly subdividing the sphere into triangles in Figure 2.4. This is called **triangulation**, and it can happen automatically or you can manually convert it.

Just because everything gets broken down into triangles, however, doesn't necessarily mean that we have to work in triangles. The art of modeling is much like the art of sculpting. We want to create geometry in

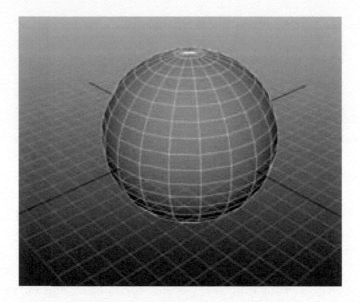

FIGURE 2.3   A sphere made of quads, or 4-sided polygons.

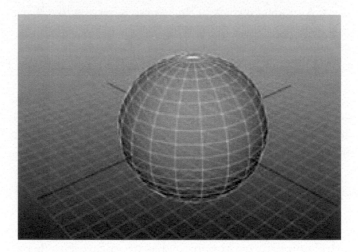

FIGURE 2.4   A sphere made of triangles, or 3-sided polygons. Quads are simply two triangles, without the triangle edge showing.

a nice, fluid, organic manner. Moving a bunch of triangles around doesn't sound very fun, does it? (See Figure 2.5.)

Figure 2.5 is comprised of many quads, nicely and evenly spaced. This is what we call a **mesh**. It is called that because it resembles a fine mesh cloth. Now, if we display it in triangles as in Figure 2.6, it becomes much

FIGURE 2.5 **(SEE COLOR INSERT)** Minnow Pete, modeled by the author.

FIGURE 2.6 **(SEE COLOR INSERT)** A lower polygon, triangulated version of Minnow Pete.

more confusing to the eye (for the sake of visualization, I have reduced the amount of polygons).

The reason for this is that it loses that nice flowing surface appearance, and the triangles ruin the visual directional flow. It is very hard to work with only triangles, and for that reason, modeling is generally done in quads when possible. Oftentimes, in modeling, when exporting to different formats, the models are automatically converted into triangles. When you import this model into another program, these triangles make it very difficult to edit the model in any reasonable manner; it is very difficult to de-triangulate a 3D model, while it only requires the click of a button to triangulate it.

FIGURE 2.7   Five-sided polygons shown without hidden triangles.

FIGURE 2.8   Hidden triangles now showing.

A polygon can have as many sides as you want it to. The caveat here is that everything is always broken down into triangles in the end. As in Figures 2.7 and 2.8, the five-sided polygon is really a collection of triangles that are being hidden.

If the polygon is planar, or all vertex positions occur in a single plane (essentially being flat), it is no big deal. The big problem comes when the polygon is non-planar, as in Figure 2.9. Maya is essentially triangulating all faces with more than three sides all the time automatically. However, if you have a quad, or four-sided polygon like Figure 2.9 that is non-planar,

FIGURE 2.9   A non-planar quad. Note the shape—it is neither concave nor convex.

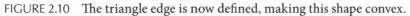
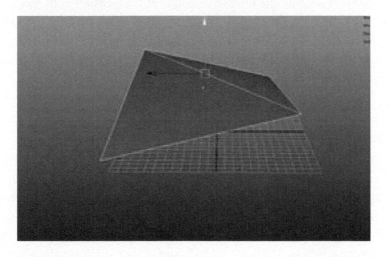

FIGURE 2.10   The triangle edge is now defined, making this shape convex.

where will that quad be divided into its two triangles? You have a quandary—it will be either convex (Figure 2.10) or concave (Figure 2.11). Because the software automatically does this for you, it can flicker between the two states when previewing. This is an important thing to resolve when modeling, especially for organic shapes where the difference can be very noticeable.

We prefer to keep all geometry in 3D to three or four sides per polygon. This is known as good **topology**. Although we want to work strictly in

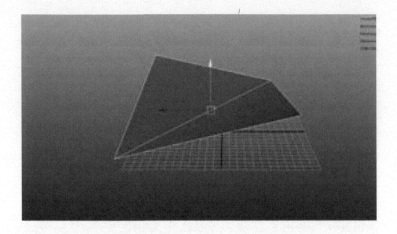

FIGURE 2.11   If the triangle edge is flipped, it becomes concave.

quads if we can, sometimes we have to use triangles to close off shapes properly. However, we never want to have polygons with more than four sides if we can help it. The only time where it is essentially OK to do so is in the case where the polygon is completely flat, in which case it will have little effect. Regardless, even in these cases it is best to convert them to four- and three-sided polygons. When and where to do this is based on the user's experience.

HOW DO I CREATE POLYGON MODELS?

Polygon Primitives

There are many ways to *create* polygonal models. The first and most common way to do so is by using **primitives**. Every 3D software program has primitives. Primitives are common shapes such as planes, cubes, spheres, and cylinders that save time by providing a starting point for various 3D models. The nice thing about primitives is that they have **parameters**, or values, that can be changed, edited, and tweaked before the geometry itself is touched. All primitives have the ability to be subdivided in various ways to increase the amount of detail available for editing the shape. We could definitely model all of this stuff ourselves if we wanted to waste the time and energy, but there is no reason to keep reinventing the wheel, so to speak. One of the nice things about working with computers is that commonly needed tasks are always compiled into easier, automated features. Primitives are so important because they offer you the speed and flexibility of generating commonly used 3D shapes with the ability to change the basic construction quickly using **history**.

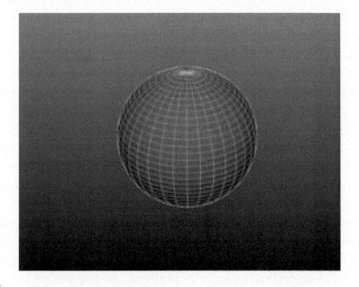

FIGURE 2.12   A polygon primitive sphere.

You can see in Figure 2.12 that I have created a primitive sphere. This sphere can have as many subdivisions in both the vertical and horizontal as I choose which I can change by accessing the **input node**, shown here in my **history**. History is a very convenient way of working with models because it allows you to go back along the things you have done and tweak them later. One thing to note is that once you change the shape node of a primitive object by moving the vertices around, it will completely destroy the positions of those vertices if you decide to go back and change how

FIGURE 2.13   The input node allows changes to the shape to be made, as long as the history is intact.

many polygons are generated by increasing the subdivisions. You will have to do that on top of the primitive in the history "stack." It is called a stack because it is like a stack. Operations happen on top of previous operations. You can clear the history at any point and convert your object into an independent polygon object. This is often done frequently in order to clear out any possible errors and speed up interactivity, which tends to slow down when there are too many operations being calculated.

Notice I have created a primitive cylinder (Figure 2.14). I can edit or adjust the values of the primitive in the history, changing the amount of subdivisions and the size and radius of creation. I am adding more divisions in the horizontal so that I have more detail available to adjust the shape of the object. Each horizontal slice of vertices offers me more ability to tweak the shape of the object. Polygons are essentially linear, which means that you need several points in order to generate a smooth appearance. Generally, you need a minimum of five points to generate the appearance of a curve, as seen in Figure 2.16. The five points create a curved appearance, although more points would improve the rounded look. As you can see, polygons tend to look very angular. Keep this in mind when we look at non-uniform rational b-splines (NURBS) surfaces.

Some other primitive shapes to look for in the creation of a polygon are text objects, which will generate 3D text for you very quickly, and generally have a plethora of creation options. Text is a very complex thing to create from the ground up, so most 3D programs have a simple interface for typing in text and generating polygon geometry from it.

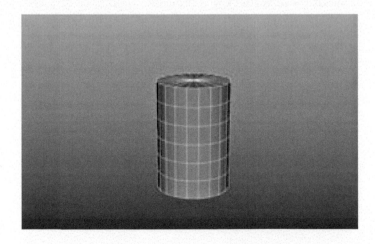

FIGURE 2.14   A primitive cylinder with several divisions added along the height.

FIGURE 2.15 The input node for the cylinder. Each primitive type will have different options.

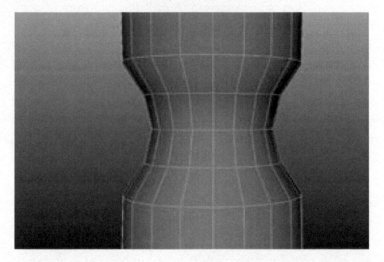

FIGURE 2.16 Adding more points allows more control over the shape with greater detail.

Point-to-point creation is another way to create your initial polygonal model. Point-to-point creation isn't nearly as quick or easy as creating primitives and editing them, but it is useful in various places. The point-to-point operation leaves a vertex every place you click the mouse, connecting the current vertex to the previous vertex with an edge and filling in the space between the first three points with a triangle. Each subsequent point clicked will create another triangle, which will be filled in until completed. In Figure 2.17, I have created a point-to-point outline of a staircase.

FIGURE 2.17   The shape of a staircase, drawn point by point.

I then use a function called **extrude** to pull the two-dimensional shape into a three-dimensional one (more on this function later).

Most software programs will end up creating this polygon as a multi-sided face and not triangulating it, like Figure 2.18. However, in reality, it will look like Figure 2.19 to the software handling the geometry. The triangles are simply hidden from your view. Notice how uneven the division of triangle is? Oftentimes it is far better to have an even distribution of triangles, even if it means adding more. When modeling polygonal geometry, we strive to have even distribution of polygons as well as economy

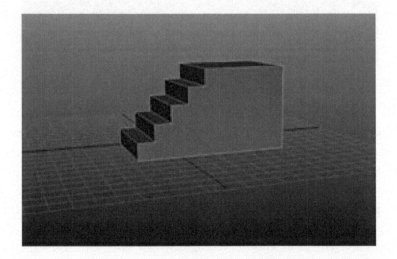

FIGURE 2.18   The staircase is made 3 dimensional by using the extrude action.

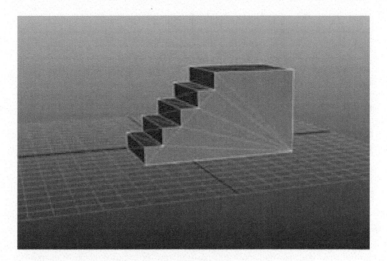

FIGURE 2.19 The triangles on the staircase being displayed. All objects are always broken down into triangles automatically.

of polygons. Sometimes one is more important than the other is. It will largely depend on the circumstances.

HOW DO I EDIT POLYGON MODELS?

Sub-Object Editing

There are literally hundreds of ways to edit polygons, and each software package has its own unique set of tools and actions to do so. More important than how to edit polygons is the question: What are you trying to model? What kind of object is it? Inanimate and simple? Or organic and complex? Is it symmetrical or branching? I could go on like this for pages, but I hope that you get the gist of it. Every type of object has its own set of challenges, and likewise a series of possible approaches. In this book, we will study three basic modeling techniques: basic building, curve-based modeling, and organic modeling. There are more techniques than this, but this covers the basics, and knowing all three you can cover anything you are given to model. When you are first modeling an object and learning how polygons work, it is best to start with something simple.

Chamfer and Bevel

Chamfer and **bevel** are two operations that do similar things, just in slightly different contexts. Essentially, they take sharp corners and make them rounded. **Chamfer** uses a vertex and **bevel** uses an edge. Look at

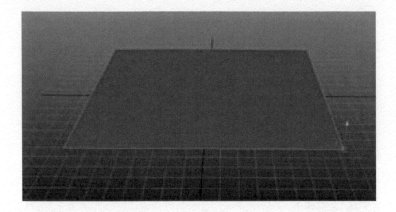

FIGURE 2.20   Selecting the corner to chamfer.

FIGURE 2.21   The chamfered vertex becomes two vertices.

Figure 2.20. You can see a polygon plane (which is actually two triangles but we are displaying it as a quad). I have selected one of the vertices and chosen the **chamfer** action from the Edit Mesh menu in Maya. You can see in Figure 2.21 that the corner vertex was converted into two vertices. This is pretty much exactly what chamfer does—it turns each vertex selected into two separate vertices, in effect rounding out a sharp corner. When I chamfer all of the vertices in this plane at once, it will round out all selected corners uniformly.

Bevel is an operation that works in a similar manner, but it rounds out an edge. In Figure 2.23, I have selected the edge of a cube. In order for bevel to work properly, there must be at least three faces attached to this

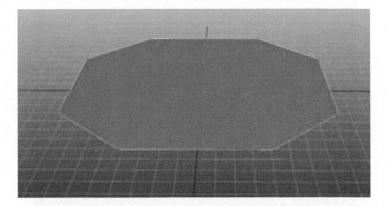

FIGURE 2.22   All of the chamfers have been done simultaneously to keep them even.

FIGURE 2.23   The edge to be beveled.

edge. When I bevel the edge, you can see in Figure 2.24 that the edge becomes rounded, effectively creating more faces in order to do so. In Figures 2.25 and 2.26, I have done this operation in Maya to all the vertical edges simultaneously in order to make them all even. If I do this operation to each edge separately, it will not be even due to the way the bevel is calculated. In Figure 2.27, you can see that it is possible to increase the amount of divisions that are created when beveling the edge, which results in a smoother corner (at the expense of extra polygons).

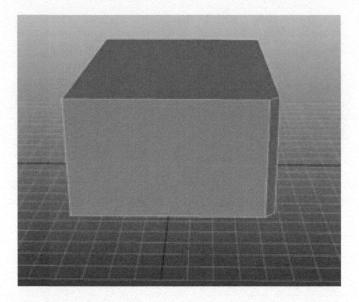

FIGURE 2.24 The resulting bevel.

FIGURE 2.25 In order to keep the edges beveled evenly, all of the horizontal edges should be selected at once.

FIGURE 2.26   The resulting beveled edges on the cube.

FIGURE 2.27   Adding more divisions to the bevel will make the edges much smoother.

Extrude

Extrude gets its own section because it is such a powerful tool in modeling. Extrude can be done on a vertex, an edge, or a face, but primarily this operation is done on faces. Extrude "pulls out" the vertex, edge, or face of a polygon while creating connecting faces that create a 3D shell around your component. It is far easier to illustrate this with pictures than with words, so you will see in Figures 2.28 through 2.33 an example of an extruded vertex, edge, and face, respectively.

Extrusions are very important in modeling because it is the only way to create branching geometry. Branching geometry is essential in creating organic shapes, like a human torso or a piece of coral. When making extrusions, most 3D tools allow you to choose between generating shells for each selected face and generating a single shell for connected faces. In Figure 2.34, I have selected four faces and extruded them, keeping the shell connected between them (in Maya, this is done by turning on "keep faces together" in the Edit Mesh window). In Figure 2.35, I have selected four faces and turned the "keep faces together" option off, which creates an individual shell of polygons for each face. This is an important feature because it is necessary to create shapes with multiple branches, like a squid's tentacles or a human hand.

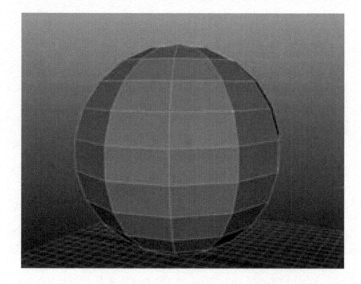

FIGURE 2.28   Vertex for extrusion selected.

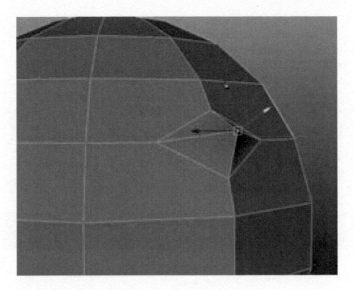

FIGURE 2.29   Vertex extruded.

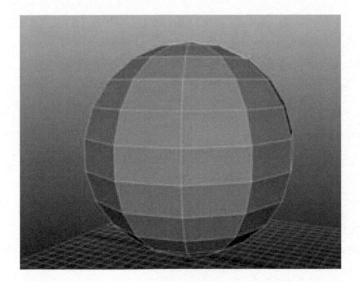

FIGURE 2.30   Edges selected for extrusion.

FIGURE 2.31   Edges extruded.

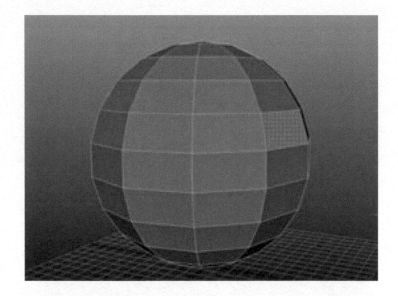

FIGURE 2.32   Face selected.

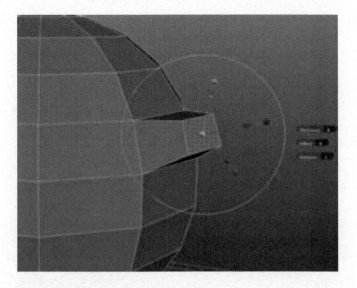

FIGURE 2.33   The face extruded.

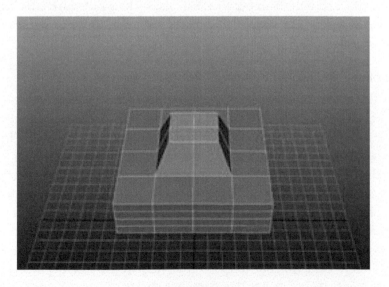

FIGURE 2.34   Faces extruded as a single shell.

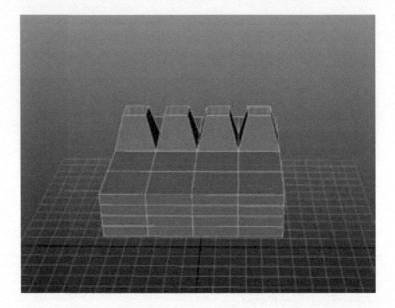

FIGURE 2.35 Faces extruded with independent shells (great for things like fingers and tentacles).

Extrusions also let you take simple shapes, such as our 2D staircase in Figure 2.17, and pull them out to 3D shells, such as in Figure 2.18. This is the best way to make simple 3D objects with non-uniform shapes (like those stairs).

Combining and Merging Multiple Polygon Objects

Thus far in our learning of polygons, we have been dealing with objects that are all connected. This means that there is a contiguous connection of the vertices in our object, which is generally known as a **shell**. This is not always necessary, however, and you can have a single object with multiple shells. To understand how to **merge** vertices and create **bridges**, we must first learn how to combine two objects. You can select two independent objects in your software package and choose a command that combines them. All this does is take both shells and put them under the same transform node. Remember when we learned how all of the components are children of the transform node? Well, here we are simply putting both objects' components under the same parent transform. This is the only way we will be able to apply operations between their components. You can see in Figure 2.36 I have combined two separate objects, which were

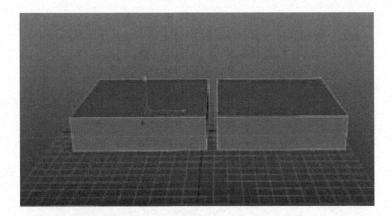

FIGURE 2.36 The two objects to merge/bridge.

cubes made from primitives. These have now become a single object, and I can then apply the next two operations, **merge** and **bridge**, to them.

Merge is a tool that works on vertices, sometimes known as "weld." Essentially, you will select two vertices (Figure 2.37) and choose to merge or "weld" them together (Figure 2.38). This will combine them into a single vertex. It is also possible to merge multiple vertices together by a certain threshold, which is very useful when multiple vertices are set up to be connected to one another (such as mirroring geometry when using symmetrical modeling).

FIGURE 2.37 Vertices are selected for welding.

FIGURE 2.38 Vertices have been welded together.

Bridging is the creation of a "bridge" polygon between two selected edges. It allows the user to connect to parts of a model that are not previously connected. You can see in Figure 2.39 I have selected two edges for bridging. In Maya, you cannot create a bridge unless it is a border edge, which means that it has a side without a connection to a face. For this reason, you can clearly see that both of the inner faces of the cubes have been deleted for the purpose of this demonstration. Some other software programs do not have this limitation, and you may bridge any two selected edges together. In Figure 2.41, you can see that multiple divisions are possible with the bridging operation, as are other adjustments such as taper and twist.

Advanced Polygon Modeling Tools

When working with polygon models, there are several methods to insert polygons into existing polygons for adding more detail. These are essential tools in the modeling process because they allow the modeler to increase detail in certain areas while leaving other areas with less detail.

The slice/scalpel/split tool is the basic foundation for creating more geometry in an existing model. There are several terms for it because various software programs call it different things. However, they all effectively perform the same function, which is to cut a single face into multiple faces

FIGURE 2.39 The two top edges are selected for bridging.

FIGURE 2.40 The two edges bridged.

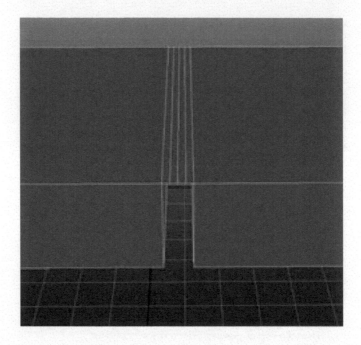

FIGURE 2.41　You can choose to have multiple segments for a bridge.

by clicking on it. I am using Maya as an example, and in it, I am using the interactive split tool, but this is available in almost all polygon modeling software packages. This tool allows you to click on an edge of a polygon and insert a vertex into that edge. Each subsequent click will create another vertex on another edge and generate an edge in between those two vertices. In Figure 2.42, I have a polygon into which I have cut a face using the interactive split tool. You can see how the split has occurred in the top face, leaving two more vertices and an extra edge. One important note about splitting an edge like this is that it leaves a vertex in the middle of the opposing edge. This is known as a "T-Edge," and you can clearly see that the side edge of the cube now has an extra face due to this new vertex. In Figures 2.43 and 2.44, you can see how the 3D software triangulates the resulting faces differently. Figure 2.43 shows an even distribution of space for the triangulation while Figure 2.44 shows an uneven distribution of space in triangulation. While this may seem unimportant when dealing with a planar face, it is an extremely important distinction when the face is non-planar. It is generally considered good topology to resolve such issues by manually triangulating the faces and maintaining even spacing as much as possible.

FIGURE 2.42   The split being made in the top face.

FIGURE 2.43   Even triangulation on one side.

Another way to increase the amount of polygons locally is to add divisions (sometimes known as subdivide) to a polygon face. You can subdivide a single face as many times as you want, and it will only add detail to the selected face. In Figure 2.45 I have selected the top face of the cube, and in Figure 2.46 I have subdivided it once. Figure 2.47 shows it being

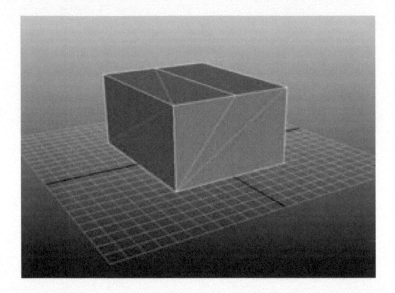

FIGURE 2.44   Uneven triangulation on the other side.

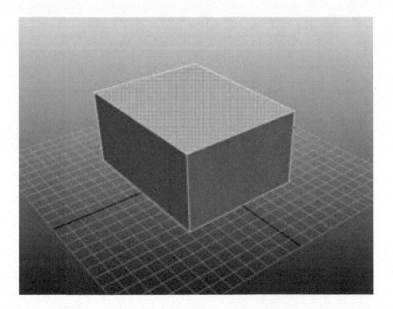

FIGURE 2.45   Face selected for subdivision.

FIGURE 2.46   Face subdivided once.

FIGURE 2.47   Face subdivided twice.

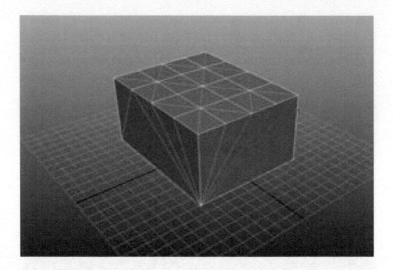

FIGURE 2.48   Resulting triangulation. Notice the unevenness.

subdivided twice. Keep in mind that the more times you subdivide a single polygon, the more T-face will occur in the surrounding faces. Those resulting triangles will most likely not be even, as you can see in Figure 2.48.

Oftentimes, a many-sided face will need to have an even distribution of triangles. Most triangulation of multi-sided faces, such as the 12-sided face shown in Figure 2.49, is incredibly uneven. You can see the natural triangulation of this geometry in Figure 2.50, where the triangles all form uneven strips to a single vertex on one of the corners. This creates a very uneven flow of triangles for the total face surface area, which can cause major problems down the road (especially in the area of UV texture mapping). What we really want for this face is to have a center vertex that acts as the crux around which the face can be evenly divided, forming a "pie" shape as shown in Figure 2.51. The operation **poke face** does this easily, creating a vertex in the center of the selected face and dividing the rest into triangles.

Smoothing

Smoothing faces or entire models is a very common polygon-editing tool. Smoothing works by increasing the number of faces in a polygon model and rounding those resulting faces out. In Figure 2.52 you can see a cube selected, and in Figure 2.53 you can see that same cube after running smooth on it. Figure 2.54 has that same cube smoothed again. Notice how the square edges get rounder and rounder as the smoothness increases?

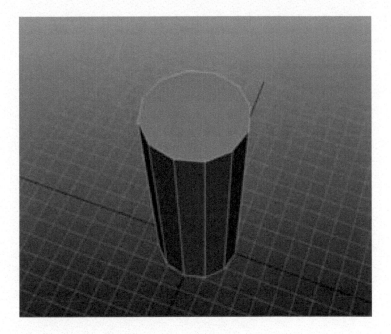

FIGURE 2.49   Twelve-sided faces for 3D object.

FIGURE 2.50   Automatic triangulation of face.

FIGURE 2.51   Poke face applied. Notice the even distribution of triangles.

FIGURE 2.52   Polygon cube before running a smooth operator.

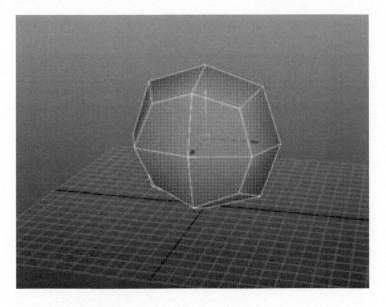

FIGURE 2.53 Smoothing the cube, with 1 iteration.

FIGURE 2.54 Smoothing the cube, with 2 iterations.

FIGURE 2.55   Three vertices are needed to create a curved appearance.

This is because of an important aspect of turning a flat edge into a rounded edge. If you have three vertices, such as you see in Figure 2.55, you can move the center one offset from the other two and it will create a shape like you see in Figure 2.56. Double your geometry and offset the other two vertices, and you will have an even rounder appearance, as in Figure 2.57. Smoothing geometry does this operation automatically across

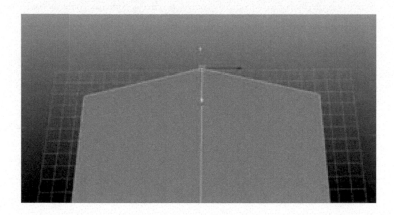

FIGURE 2.56   By generating a triangular shape, the semblance of a curve can begin to be created.

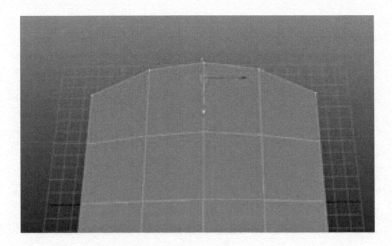

FIGURE 2.57   More vertices allow greater curvature.

all of the faces that you select, effectively allowing you to model a relatively low-resolution model and then automatically converting it into a much smoother, high-resolution one. In Figure 2.58 you can see the low resolution of a fish character model for a game in progress. Figure 2.59 is that same model with a global smooth operation on it.

FIGURE 2.58 **(SEE COLOR INSERT)**   Original, low-poly models by author.

FIGURE 2.59 **(SEE COLOR INSERT)** Same models after smoothing. The angular edges are gone, but the polygon count has almost tripled! Always strive to use the least polygons possible when modeling.

EXERCISE: MODELING WITH POLYGON TOOLS

In this exercise, you will learn some simple, but essential polygon modeling tools. This tutorial, along with all the other exercises, is meant to go hand in hand with the videos on the website, so please make sure to use them concurrently. It is far more effective to show you all the clicks, tools, and options in a video with audio while describing what I am doing than it is to write every last action down! Let's begin.

Remember that simple staircase we built with polygon primitives? Let's try it again, only this time we can do it with pure polygonal modeling tools (no primitives allowed!). The first tool we will use is the **create polygon tool**. The create polygon tool is a simple tool, which allows us to "draw" a polygon by clicking to slap down a vertex, which will always be connected to the last vertex set down. The first and last vertices will always be connected when the tool is completed, by hitting the "enter" key. Hitting "enter" while in any tool automatically ends the tool by entering the input into the parameters. A tool in Maya is an operation that requires some user input before completing, while an action happens at once, after applying it. Some actions, however, can have a manipulator, which can be accessed and edited after the action has been performed (more on this later).

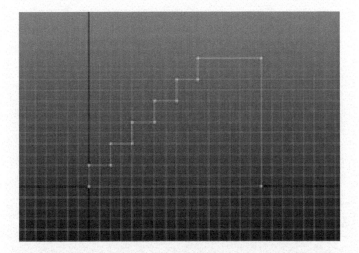

FIGURE 2.60   Snap the points to the grid using the create polygon tool.

Step 1: Create Polygon Tool

The create polygon tool can snap its vertices to the grid or points by using the snap options, which will ensure that each vertex is aligned with that grid point or points. Change your view to orthographic side and use the grid snap to create a polygon with the create polygon tool as illustrated in Figure 2.60. The side view will ensure that all points snap to the grid and that our staircase is aligned with the world properly.

Step 2: Extruding the Object

Now you can return to the perspective view in order to see what you have created. Don't forget to turn shaded mode ("4" key) on to see the polygonal face colored in! We seem to have a staircase here, but it looks like somebody sliced off the end like a piece of bread. We don't have any depth! The way to create depth from a flat polygon is to use the Edit Mesh > Extrude action. An extrude "pulls" out the selected polygonal face and creates what is known as a "shell" or connected faces with depth. The face you extrude is duplicated and connected to new faces to give it depth. Figure 2.61 is an image of what happens when you extrude the polygon we just created. Extrude is one of the actions that has its own manipulator, which allows you to transform the new face as you create it, in the 3D view. Move the translate Z outward and you will see the staircase magically create depth, turning it into a bona fide 3D object.

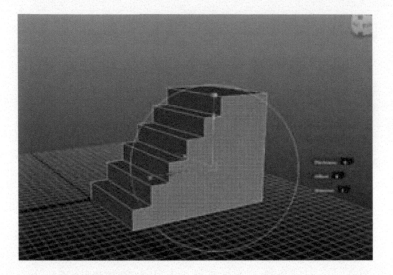

FIGURE 2.61 Don't forget to move the extruded face out from its position—it doesn't happen by default, which causes many of my students infinite grief when they think that they haven't created the extrusion and end up having two sets of faces right on top of each other! It completely whacks out your geometry and makes it very hard to continue a model down the road.

Step 3: Beveling Edges

Next, we will perform an action known as beveling. Beveling is taking a hard edge and "rounding" it out. Many hard edges on objects such as walls, floors, and furniture, and structural items such as buildings, stairs, and other manufactured items look unnatural if left with sharp edges. Beveling is an action in Maya, found under Edit Mesh > Bevel, which will perform a rounding action on any selected edge. To select the sub-object polygon edge of the stairs object, you can right-click over the object and hold, which will bring up the marking menu. Select "edge" and you will then be able to select the edges of the polygon. Alternately, you can hit the "f10" key, which is the shortcut to select sub-objects of type "edge." Once you have selected the lip edges of the stairs model, open up the bevel action options (which will be a small box next to the menu item). Choose a width of .1 and 1 segment. Click on apply, and you will see the result as in Figure 2.63.

Congratulations! You have now created a modestly complex polygonal staircase with a few modest tools and actions. Physical structures like architectural elements are a great place to learn polygonal modeling because they are flat on many surfaces, which allows you to see things in

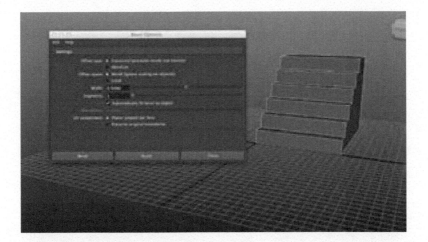

FIGURE 2.62   Preparing the bevels.

FIGURE 2.63   Resulting bevels.

a solid, structural way. When you move on to organic modeling, things begin to get a lot more difficult due to the complex curvature and surface flow.

Things learned in this exercise:

- Create polygon tool

- Polygonal extrusion

- Sub-object selection (edge)

- Edge beveling

CHAPTER 3

NURBS and Curve-Based Geometry

QUESTIONS TO BE ANSWERED

What are curves? *NURBS, Bézier*

How are curves represented in 3D? *Bézier Handles, CVs, EPs*

How are surfaces generated in 3D? *Lofting and all derivative actions*

What are the properties of a NURBS surface? What is tessellation? *Why NURBS is different from polygons*

What are the advantages of NURBS? *Surface-based modeling*

What are the disadvantages of NURBS modeling?

How can NURBS be converted into polygons? *Conversion parameters and their meanings*

Now that we have gone through the basic elements of polygonal-based modeling, we need to learn the second major type of modeling methodology—curve-based modeling.

Usually known as NURBS modeling, although the curves themselves need not actually be NURBS curves, curve-based modeling is a very different method of generating geometry. The resulting geometry is known as a *surface* or a *skin* and although it is ultimately converted into polygons, it is a very different beast from polygonal modeling.

Surfaces are **adaptive**, which means that they can be broken down into as many subdivisions as necessary to produce smooth results. This is very different from polygonal **smoothing** because it constantly changes the number of triangles generated based on various parameters. However, before we can understand surfaces, we really need to understand curves and their properties.

WHAT IS A CURVE?

In terms of computer graphics, curves are entities that have a shape and properties based on points in space. Those points are called **control points** or **control vertices (CVs)**. These points on a curve are what determine the shape of that curve. There are different types of curves, which use different calculations to determine the shape, and therefore have different controls over that curve. The two main types of curves are **Bézier curves** and **NURBS curves**. Every type of graphics program, including Adobe Illustrator, Photoshop, and After Effects, has some implementation of these types of curves and editing capabilities. Generally speaking, 2D curves use Bézier and 3D curves use NURBS implementation, although Autodesk Maya is now fully supporting Bézier curves in its 3D surface implementation. We will be studying NURBS implementation as a rule for 3D surface creation.

When understanding curves as a general concept, the important thing to keep in mind is this: A computer can't really draw a curve. In fact, a computer has no real understanding of a "curve" in the sense that we understand it. A computer, by its nature, can only understand points in space and straight lines drawn between them. In Figure 3.1 you can see an arc curve created in Maya. The curve *looks* like a curve to our eye; however, as you can see in Figure 3.2, it is actually a bunch of straight lines, drawn in between points, which appear to be a curve from far away because our eye cannot distinguish between a lot of straight lines and a curve when the distance is too great. Our brain actually fills in the details and makes it look like a curve.

Now, if we want to create a curve in 3D, we must draw a whole bunch of points close together, and draw straight lines through those points. If you have enough of those points, the line drawn between them will appear to be a curve to the human eye, even though it is really a bunch of straight lines. Bézier and NURBS curves are essentially a mathematical method of generating large amounts of points in space from only a few main control points. This is an important part of curve-based modeling because

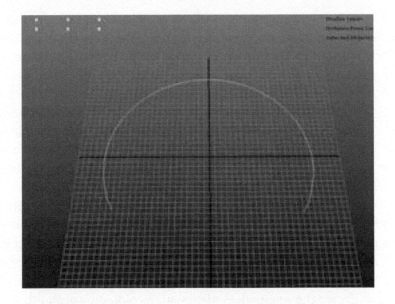

FIGURE 3.1 Simple arc curves.

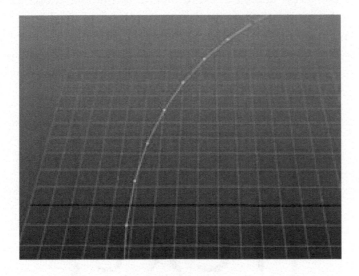

FIGURE 3.2 A closer look reveals what is really going on—it isn't a curve at all!

it means that the curve information we create from a few points is completely adaptive. Adaptive means that we can subdivide the spaces between the main control vertices or control points as many times as we need to in order to make it appear smooth. The computer draws the curve to the screen using pixels, but because the pixels are generated by the equation of the curve it can change the amount of pixels generated depending on how much of the screen the curve is taking up. That is to say, the number of pixels can increase or decrease to adapt to the needs of the moment, which ensures that the resulting image is always smooth. This **adaptive rendering** (or converting into pixels) of the curve is the heart of vector-based graphics, which is essentially the 2D version of surface-based modeling. A good example of something commonly using vector graphics is computer text. No matter how much you zoom in, the resolution remains the same. If the text were based on pixels, it would get fuzzier and fuzzier if you zoomed into it.

To illustrate this concept, let's look at a couple of images. In Figure 3.3 you can see an example of a vector-based text word I created in Photoshop. In Figure 3.4 I scaled this same text much larger, which you can see results in the rounded edges of the letter "e" being just as smooth as they were at a smaller size. This is because of the concept of adaptive rendering. The pixels, which are the square dots filled with a color, are constantly being updated to be drawn inside the lines of the text. When I **rasterize** the image, or convert it completely into pixel information, I lose the ability to adaptively convert the text into as many pixels as I need and suddenly the closer you get to the text (or the more you scale it), the more you can clearly see the boxes (or pixels) that make up the text as it is displayed. The sides no longer continue to get smoother on the letter "e" but now appear jagged, as in Figure 3.5.

FIGURE 3.3   Vector-based text.

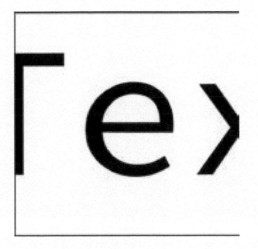

FIGURE 3.4   Vector-based text enlarged.

FIGURE 3.5   Rasterized text enlarged. Note the jagged edges.

WHAT ARE NURBS CURVES AND HOW DO THEY WORK?

NURBS curves are special curves that use "control points" to determine the shape of the curve. Each NURBS curve consists of multiple control points and a curve drawn between them. There are two basic types of NURBS curves: linear and smooth.

Also called a 1-degree curve, a linear curve is where the lines are drawn straight through the CVs and there is no actual "curve." Figure 3.6 is an example of a 1-degree or linear curve with four CVs.

Also called a 3-degree surface, a smooth curve is where there is a curve determined through the CVs. Notice that in a 3-degree curve it requires

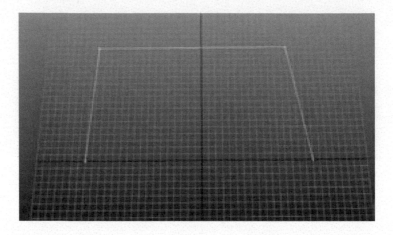

FIGURE 3.6 Example of a 1-degree or linear curve with four control vertices (CVs).

four CVs to generate a single curve or **span**—the first and second CV, and then two more. Therefore, every span consists of a number of CVs equal to the degree of the curve –1. There are 5- and 7-degree curves, which are used when much higher degrees of accuracy are called for (like in designing industrial molds and microchip circuitry); however, 3 is the usual standard. This means that you cannot have what we consider a "curve" until you have at least four CVs, which will then equal a span. When you have a longer, more complex curve, what is really happening is that you have multiple spans being strung together. Notice that in a 3-degree or higher

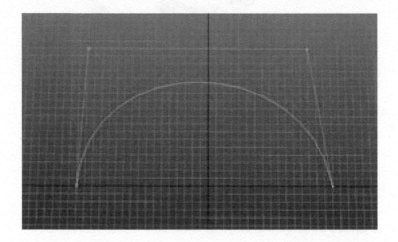

FIGURE 3.7 Four control vertices have formed a curved line between them, based on some "math stuff"—note the linear version of the curve is always still there (known as the hull).

curve, the CVs do not lie on the curve itself—they exist slightly outside of it. This is a lot harder to edit than polygonal vertices, which lie exactly where the edges intersect. In Figure 3.7 you can see the same curve as Figure 3.6; however, this curve is a cubic, or 3-degree curve, so it has a curved shape instead of a linear one. Notice that the 1-degree shape is still there in a cubic curve, only now it is known as the **hull,** or linear connection between the CVs. Also, note that the CVs of a 3-degree curve don't lie on the curve, but rather off the curve that they are representing.

Curves can be **open, closed,** or **periodic.** Periodic and closed are very similar, in that the end and beginning knots are in the exact same place; however, there are some slight differences mathematically and periodic is the standard type used for any curve that has the same beginning and ending place. Technically speaking, a curve must have a beginning CV and an ending CV, so the curve can never be truly a circle—it just appears to be one. For this reason, a surface generated from curves can never be truly "seamless." It will always have a seam somewhere on the edge. In Figure 3.8, you can see a NURBS curve that is open. In Figure 3.9, you can see that I have changed it to periodic by choosing Close Curve.

Curves are generated by the CVs, but they have several other sub-objects that determine their shape and properties (just keep in mind that these

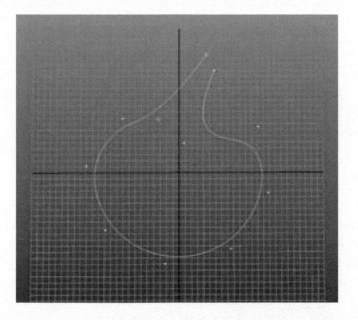

FIGURE 3.8   This curve is open because it has a different beginning and end.

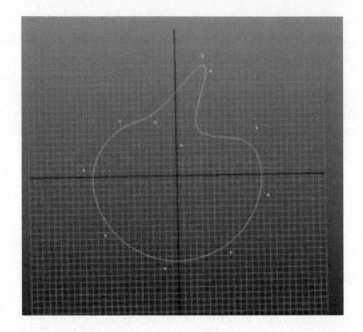

FIGURE 3.9   This is a periodic curve, in which the beginning and end are the same.

are always derived from the CVs in the way that polygon vertices control the shape of polygonal geometry). **Hulls** are the straight lines drawn between CVs (even when the curves are smooth or 3 degrees) and **edit points** are the places where curves with more than one **span** are attached. Very rarely, however, are curves edited with hulls or edit points. Rather, they are indicators of the curve shape and complexity. In Figure 3.10, you can see the Edit Point of a cubic curve, where they lay on the curve, as opposed to the CVs, which are off the curve.

A **curve point** is a sub-object that cannot be edited, rather it is a derived object, which gets its values from another object. In this case, the curve point derives its position from the curve—it can be ANY point that lies on the curve. This is a huge difference from the **control vertex**, which lies off the curve. The Control Vertex determines the shape of the curve. The curve point is a position that lies on the curve (determined by the position of those control vertices), which you will then use in operations which **detach the curve** at that point, or **insert knots** (adding more CV's) in that place. **Inserting a knot** inserts a control vertex at the location of the curve point. In Figure 3.11, I have selected a curve point, and in Figure 3.12 I have inserted an extra CV where that selection was.

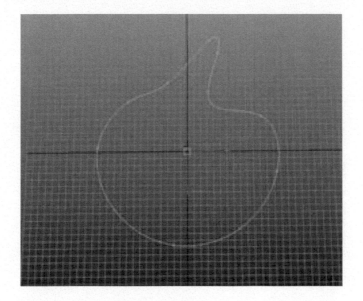

FIGURE 3.10   Edit points lay on the curve.

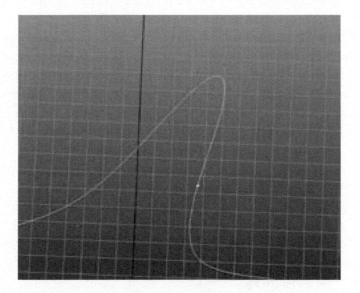

FIGURE 3.11   Curve point is selected on the curve.

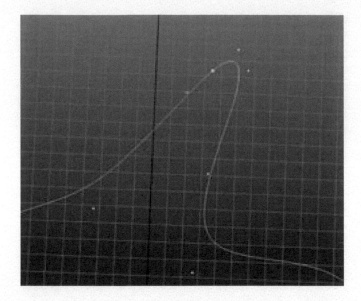

FIGURE 3.12   A new control vertex is created where the curve point was. Note how it does not lay on the curve, but slightly off the curve (because this is a cubic curve).

HOW DO YOU CREATE NURBS CURVES?

You can use various methods to create NURBS curves. The most common method of creating curves is by laying down CVs by snapping to the grid using a Create CV Curve Tool, but maintaining the curve degree to 1. This makes the curves easily controlled at first, allowing the placement of the points to be symmetrical and exact. The curve can then be converted (see editing NURBS curves) into 3-degree curves after the fact. The reason for creating the curve as a 1-degree and then converting to 3 degrees is that it is very hard to control the shape of a curve with placement of CVs in 3 degrees because it requires 4 of them to define the shape of the curve. If you create the curve in 1 degree and convert to 3 degrees, you can be much more accurate during the initial creation.

There are also "pencil drawing tools" that allow you to create curves by drawing a shape. These curves are generally poorly created and uneven in the CV placement, but the ability to **rebuild** a curve makes this a reasonable method of generating curves as well (see the next section for an explanation of **rebuilding** curves).

HOW DO I EDIT NURBS CURVES?

Editing a NURBS curve is largely dependent on what you need to do with it. Since we still have not gotten to the *useful* part of a NURBS curve, we still have to think about it in a theoretical sense more than a practical sense. The simplest method of editing a curve is to transform the CVs.

Each CV has its own independent transform, which can be changed just like a polygonal vertex. These changes in the CVs will change the shape of the resulting curve, but not always exactly the way you intend! Because a 3-degree curve requires four CVs to form a smooth curve, changes in a single CV will not always give you the control over the shape as you might hope. Generally, you will make adjustments to all the CVs governing the curve in order to create the appearance you want.

Sometimes you will want to increase the number of CVs in a curve. You can do this in a number of ways. The simplest is to select a curve point somewhere on the curve, and choose the Insert Knot command. This will add a single CV at the selected curve point, which you can then edit to further refine that part of your curve.

Another way to increase the complexity, and one of the most important properties about NURBS curves, is known as rebuilding a curve. Rebuilding a curve is taking an existing curve and changing the number of CVs in it, while matching the shape of that curve as much as possible. This allows you to take a curve and specify how many spans and CVs it has while keeping the same basic shape. This is very important for a number of reasons (and carries over into surfaces as well). Oftentimes a curve is not uniform when you create it—the process of generating a curve with a pencil tool or the create curve tool will leave the curve with very uneven distances between the CVs of a curve. Editing the CVs manually can also tweak the total space between CVs, which is known as **parameterization**. Parameterization is the spacing between CVs on a curve or curves on a surface. It is very important for many reasons, chief among them is to provide a nice, even distribution of the sub-objects that determine the shape of your model. Without proper parameterization, it is very difficult to do things down the road, such as convert your model to polygons or texture it properly.

In Figure 3.13, I have a curve that has been drawn in with the pencil tool. Notice how uneven and inefficient the CVs are. Using the rebuild curve action, I can preserve the basic shape while ensuring that the spacing is

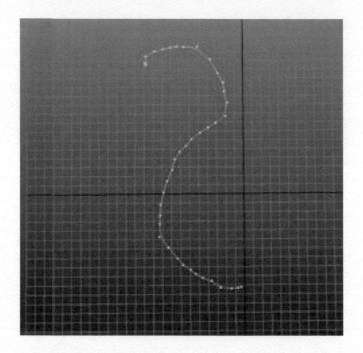

FIGURE 3.13   Notice how many CVs there are.

nice and even while drastically reducing the amount of CVs. Figure 3.14 illustrates the result of the rebuilt curve. This is a vital feature of NURBS curves and surfaces, giving the user a lot of flexibility in tweaking the shape and subsequently "smoothing" out the parameterization (or even spacing). You cannot do this with polygons!

The problem with NURBS is that the process of creating and editing them leads to very uneven parameterization. Rebuilding the curve is a good fix for this because it can retain the basic shape while creating uniform spacing between the CVs. It also allows you to reduce curves with extremely large amounts of CVs into something more editable.

Another important aspect of rebuilding curves is the ability to convert curves from 1 degree to 3 degrees. This is a very useful tool because when you create curves, initially you can be very precise about where you place the points by using a 1-degree curve. You can snap the points to a grid and then use the rebuild operation to convert your curve to a 3-degree curve, which will make it smooth. In Figure 3.15, I have created the outline of a wine glass as a 1-degree (linear) curve. Using the rebuild feature of NURBS curves, I have converted it into a smooth curve in Figure 3.16.

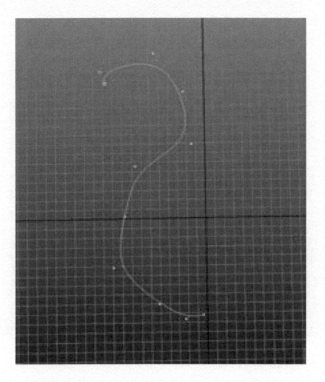

FIGURE 3.14   The same shape as in Figure 3.13, but much less CVs means less work adjusting it.

WHAT ARE NURBS CURVES USED FOR? WHAT DO I DO WITH THEM?

Now you know what a NURBS curve is and how to create it. So, what do you do with them? Because although you can create incredibly complex networks of curves, without actual geometry all you have is a bunch of curves that outline the shape of an object. This is actually a very good time to get into describing the workflow of NURBS-based modeling, which is significantly different from polygonal modeling. The purpose of NURBS is to create a network of curves that define the object you are trying to model, be it a shoe, iPhone case, or creature. The process of NURBS modeling is to define that outline with as many curves as possible, using reference images or just your talent as a digital sculptor, and then turning them into **surfaces** by stretching an imaginary **skin** or canvas between them using an operation called a **loft.** Figure 3.17 illustrates a network of curves that

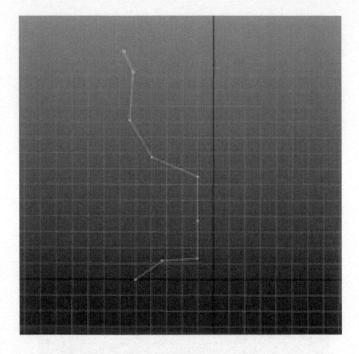

FIGURE 3.15 Created by clicking CVs in linear mode.

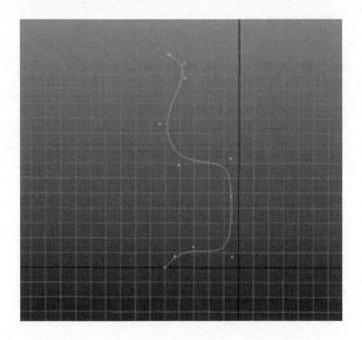

FIGURE 3.16 Rebuilt as a cubic or smooth curve using rebuild curve.

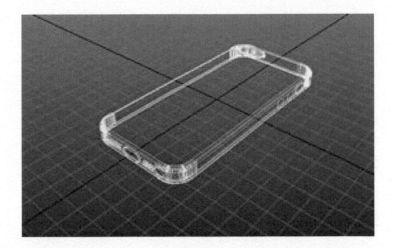

FIGURE 3.17   Curve outline of an iPhone case drawn with NURBS.

FIGURE 3.18   Surfaces have been created from the outlines, forming a solid object.

outline the complex curvature of an iPhone case, while Figure 3.18 illustrates that same network of curves that have been converted into a surface. Figure 3.19 illustrates that same NURBS surface converted into polygonal geometry.

NURBS modeling is pretty difficult and complex, with dizzying amounts of parameters, tools, options, and methodologies, but it is important to understand what all of them are *doing*. Before you get lost in a NURBS modeling program, you should know what the fundamental

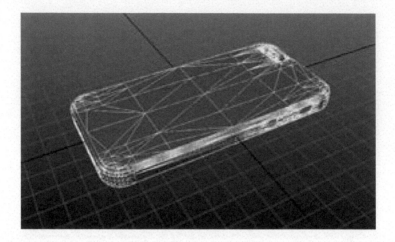

FIGURE 3.19 The polygonal version of the surfaces (in triangles). Note how there are more triangles in the areas where more detail is needed to form smooth curves.

strategy is in order to get anything out of it. You want to create a model by outlining its shape with curves and then go about creating geometry between those curves to create a 3D model. You can do all sorts of other things with NURBS curves and surfaces, but this was the original intention for using them, and this is how they are used in modeling in 99% of the cases. Part of the intention of this book is not only to give you a good foundation about how the basic understanding of how things work in 3D, but also how these things are used. Many earlier tutorials about modeling and NURBS surfaces used very clunky examples of things that were not really following the professional workflow of use. Because 3D computer graphics is such a gigantic area of knowledge, it is just as important to filter out what you don't need as is what you do!

WHAT ARE NURBS SURFACES? HOW ARE THEY CREATED?

So, we have generated the curves necessary to create our object (we will get more specific in the Exercise part of this section) and now we need to create a surface between them. First we have to understand what a **surface** is and how it works.

Remember how we talked about those vector graphics vs. bitmap graphics? And how a vector is a representative of pixels, based on how many of them need to be generated? Well, a NURBS surface is a lot like that vector. Essentially, a NURBS surface is a skin, or the space between two or more curves which is generated with an action called a **loft**. In Figure 3.20, you can see two curves with a smooth surface area being rendered in between

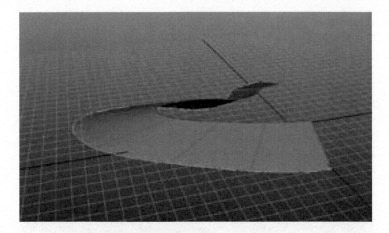

FIGURE 3.20   A loft between two curves generates this surface.

them. The surface is the smooth area in between the curves. It works by creating polygons in the area between the curves, which are then displayed to your screen as pixels, which is known as "rendering" (see Chapter 4 for more on this). The different between this NURBS surface and a straight polygonal object is that the polygon surface has a finite amount of vertices, edges, and faces; that is, each vertex is accounted for by its transform. In a NURBS surface, however, the amount of vertices and triangles are completely mutable. They are being generated in real time, as many as necessary to display the object in a perfectly smooth way, just as a curve generates enough pixels to display a smooth line. Figure 3.21 shows this same surface's polygon **tessellation** displayed. Tessellation is the dynamic conversion of a surface into polygon triangles so that they can be displayed to the screen. This is an extremely important concept to understand because it is the basis of the distinction of NURBS and polygons, which is that the NURBS are being converted into polygons continuously and adaptively, which means that the amount can be increased or decreased depending on how many are needed to make the object smooth when being displayed to the screen. This can be dynamically edited for any surface, as you can see in Figure 3.22, which is the same surface as in Figure 3.21 with the adaptive tessellation setting turned up a couple of notches. These settings can create as many polygons as necessary to create a smooth look from any distance, making NURBS the best option for objects that must be rendered at extremely high resolutions.

A **loft**, in its simplest execution, defines a space between two curves with the same amount of knots. Each span is connected to the span in the

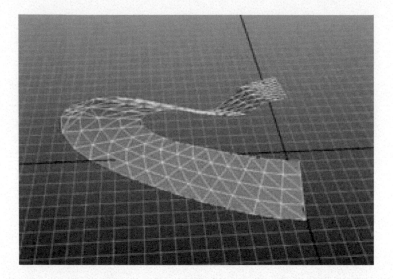

FIGURE 3.21 The tessellated version of the surface. (I have turned on "display tessellation" so you can see the surface as Maya generates the polygons from the curve information.)

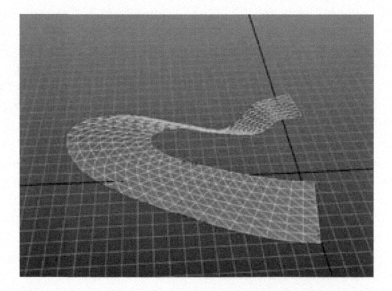

FIGURE 3.22 The same lofted surface, with the tessellation turned up a few notches.

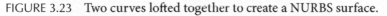

FIGURE 3.23 Two curves lofted together to create a NURBS surface.

second curve as the loft occurs. Cross-spans are created, which connect from one curve to another, based on the edit points (EPs) and the direction of the curve (where the first knot is). Although some modeling programs can loft two curves together that do not have the same number of spans, it is very unreliable and tends to make the resulting surface very uneven. Most lofts are done between curves with identical numbers of spans, and oftentimes a curve is duplicated and offset in some way to generate to a second curve. In Figure 3.23, you can see two curves, highlighted in green, which have been lofted together. In Figure 3.24, you can see the result of several curves lofted together to form a surface. These lofts were created by duplicating a single curve (which ensures that they all contain the same amount of spans and CVs, which will also be lined up to make the loft clean and even). Keep in mind that the loft is the primary method of generating a surface—all modeling techniques we use subsequently (revolve/lathe, extrusion, birail, etc.) are simply complex versions of the loft operation which are automated to make your life easier.

The NURBS surface, if there is modeling history in your software, will be dependent on the curves you used to create it. This, however, is only temporary and not necessary because when made independent (history deleted), the surface will contain all of the curves inherently as **hulls**, or an entire line of CVs. Figure 3.25 illustrates the V (or vertical) hull of a lofted surface, while Figure 3.26 illustrates a hull in the U (horizontal).

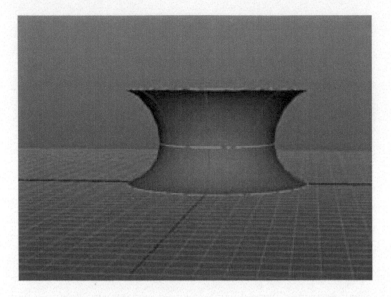

FIGURE 3.24 Multiple curves lofted together to create a cubic NURBS surface.

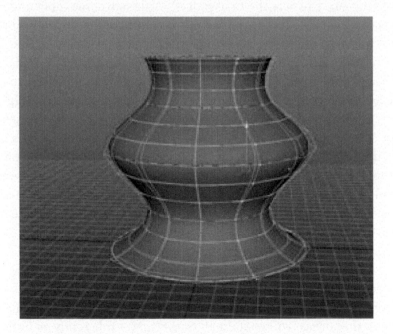

FIGURE 3.25 A hull is all of the CVs in a line on any surface. This is the V, or vertical direction.

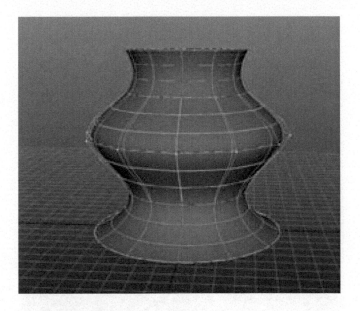

FIGURE 3.26   A hull in the U, or horizontal direction.

Those hulls will define the surface continuously, which is constantly being tessellated and displayed to the scene. So the NURBS surface has its own inherent curves that control it, as it is essentially always being lofted and displayed based on the curves of which it consists. Most modeling packages allow you to create the surfaces with a history, which will update as the shape of the curve updates. Once you make the surface independent, it will retain those initial curves as the sub-objects that construct it.

ALL NURBS surfaces are essentially flat ribbons, which are constantly being subdivided into polygons that follow the lines of the curves of which they consist. When laid out flat, they have U (horizontal) and V (vertical) space. They cannot be a "solid," or a completely closed surface on all sides, because of their basic nature. You can have a closed or periodic surface (which will happen if your lofting curves are closed or periodic), but like a curve there must be a beginning and an end, and where the two meet there will be **seam**, which you can see as in Figure 3.27. So essentially, you can fool the eye into believing that the surface is "closed," but in reality, it will still really be just a flat ribbon! The NURBS cylinder in Figure 3.27 is really a flat ribbon wrapped around a cylindrical shape and connected at the seams, which you see highlighted. Figure 3.28 shows you the two seams, split apart. If you unravel this surface, it would just be a long ribbon. It appears to us as a cylinder, however, because the beginning and end

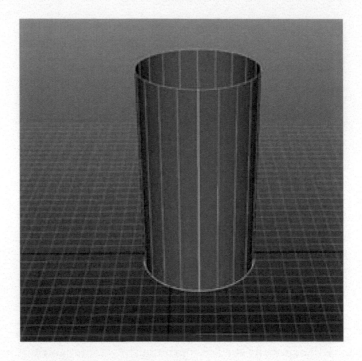

FIGURE 3.27 It looks like a closed cylinder.

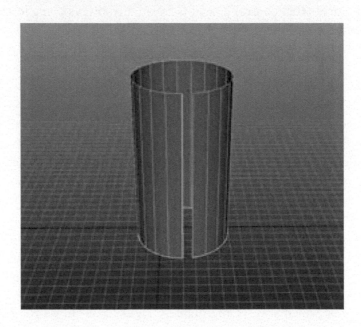

FIGURE 3.28 NURBS has fooled you into believing that the cylinder was closed! It really looks like this.

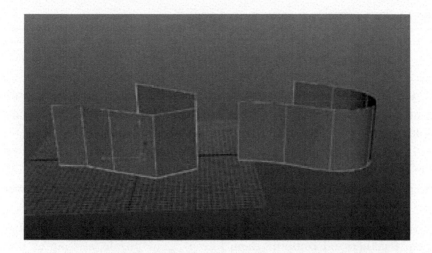

FIGURE 3.29   Linear and smooth NURBS surfaces adjacent to one another.

of the surface are moving together, fooling us into believing they are the same. To all rendered appearances, this is a cylinder, and it is how NURBS surfaces appear to be solid objects. A NURBS surface can only be closed in one direction, the U or the V, so like that flat ribbon it can never be a solid object.

If you had to model every 3D object with long ribbons that could be twisted and turned into any shape desirable, you would either have to use a big surface with a lot of extra hulls added (which can't be closed in both directions), or you would have to have many pieces, stuck together like patchwork. This problem with the nature of NURBS makes it very convenient to do certain types of modeling (like cars, or for engineering devices) and very bad for others (like organic shapes). The upside of NURBS modeling is that you can continuously subdivide the surfaces to create a smooth appearance no matter how close or far away the model is from the camera displaying it (we will visit this concept later). In addition, U and V coordinates are very easily generated with NURBS surfaces for texture mapping and other purposes (more on this in Chapter 4).

A NURBS surface behaves and is edited much like a NURBS curve, with the exception that it has curves in the U and V, which are what generate the polygons that allow you to "see" a surface at all. Any line that you select on a surface, U or V, is called an **isoparm**, which is much like a **curve point** on a curve. You can manipulate CVs on a surface, and a surface can be linear or smooth (3-degree). In a linear surface, the CVs are on the surface, while on a smooth surface the CVs are off the surface.

HOW DO I EDIT NURBS SURFACES?

You can edit NURBS surfaces a number of ways. The most common way is to use construction history and to edit the curves that generate the surfaces as much as possible, only making the surface independent when necessary. Surface shape can be edited with the transform of CVs and hulls (which just transform all the CVs of a single span in U or V). It is also possible to rebuild a surface, just like a curve, only now you have to determine both U and V parameters. Once you have worked with NURBS surfaces, you can begin to see how similar they are to NURBS curves, the only difference being that the surface is generating triangles, which are displayed on your screen.

Surfaces (as well as curves) can be **attached,** which allows you to snap them together and combine them like a jigsaw puzzle, as long as they are lined up correctly. When attaching surfaces you have to determine whether you will insert a new span in the area you intend to attach them (which will be necessary for preserving the shape if the curve is smooth). Generally, you want as few surfaces in a model as possible, and the ultimate goal is to have a single, flowing surface that has spans evenly distributed throughout. Figure 3.30 shows two NURBS surfaces before being attached, and Figure 3.31 shows them after being joined. Notice the extra span created in between.

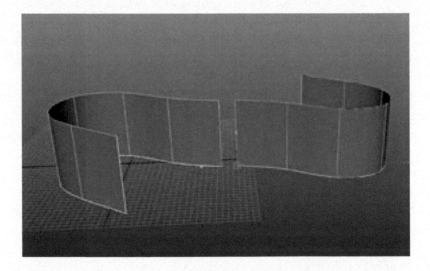

FIGURE 3.30   Two curves to be attached.

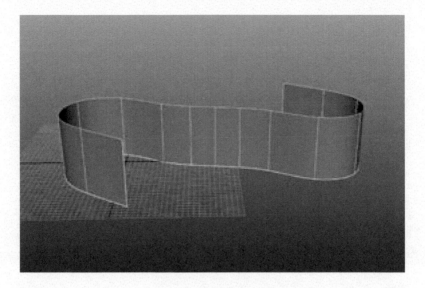

FIGURE 3.31 Curves attached, with extra spans created to blend in the attached area.

Surfaces (and curves) can also be **detached**, which splits the surface at the isoparm you have selected, effectively acting like a scalpel in either the U or V of a surface. Figure 3.32 shows an isoparm selected on a surface, and Figure 3.33 shows those surfaces split along that same isoparm, generating two distinct surfaces.

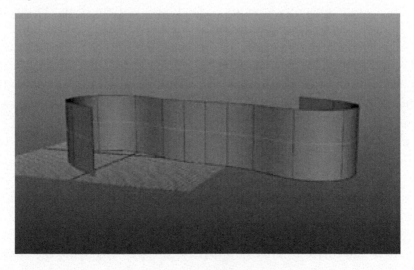

FIGURE 3.32 The isoparm selected to separate the surfaces.

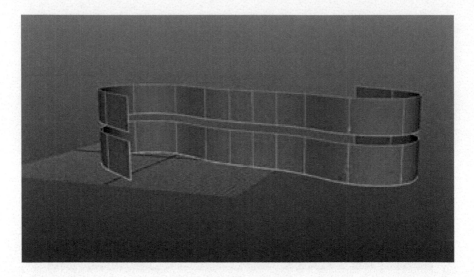

FIGURE 3.33   Two surfaces created from one by separating them along a selected isoparm.

HOW DO I CREATE NURBS SURFACES OUT OF MY CURVE OUTLINES?

The basic creation tool, the loft, has already been discussed. This, in itself, is enough to generate every surface you would ever need, if you could outline a curve for every contour of the object you are trying to create. The problem, however, is that creating a curve for every single contour on every single part of your model is tedious and slow (although this is a valid modeling method and probably the most reliable when working with NURBS). In NURBS modeling, we want to make use of some automatically generated forms of **lofting** that help in the creation of certain types of models and shapes.

Revolve, extrude, and **birail** are three tools for surface creation we will look at. It is important, however, to keep in mind that these are all just extensions of the loft, as are all other NURBS creation tools. They are operations that generate and loft together curves based on some kind of automated action.

Revolve, or in some programs a **lathe**, is a tool that takes a single profile curve and turns it into a symmetrical surface by copying the curve, duplicating it a certain number of times, rotating those duplicates around a fixed axis, and then lofting all of those duplicate curves together into a surface. While this can be done manually step by step, it is a lot easier to

FIGURE 3.34 The original profile curve to shape the wine glass.

FIGURE 3.35 The resulting wine glass surface generated by using a revolve or lathe surface creation.

click a button than to spend an hour setting it all up. Instead of doing all that work, I can create a single profile curve outlining the shape I want to create, as I have in Figure 3.34. In Figure 3.35, I have used a revolve operation. You can see how the shape of the surface generated matches my profile curve exactly, forming a symmetrical shape that is even on all sides. This is the result of that duplicating, rotating, and lofting of the original

FIGURE 3.36   Transforming this one CV can alter the entire surface shape!

profile curve, just compacted into a single operation. Because of the construction history, which is set up to keep the operation separate from the original shape, subsequent changes to the profile curve will change the shape of the NURBS object. If the construction history is turned off or deleted, the surface will become independent and it will no longer be adjustable from a single CV from a single curve. This is also an advantage of doing this operation vs. lofting the curves yourself because it allows you to make changes to a single point and have them ripple down the chain to adjust the entire surface. Notice how quick and easy this method is in creating a symmetrical surface. Figure 3.36 illustrates how changing a single CV on the initial curve can change the shape of the entire surface. It is a quick and easy way to adjust the total shape with a single point in space. We will go over this particular example in this chapter's exercise.

Extrude is a method of creating a surface similar to the polygons extrude we studied earlier, but with NURBS instead. It requires two curves—a profile curve and a path curve. If you had Play-Doh® as a kid, or own a pasta-maker now, you will understand the basic method of extruding along a path. The profile curve provides the shape of the surface, and the path curve is the tube along which it extrudes. Just like squeezing out Play-Doh or pasta from that shape, the surface will be generated and follow along the path curve based on the profile curve shape, making a

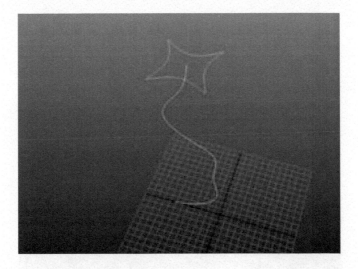

FIGURE 3.37   The star-shaped profile curve and the squiggly path curve are selected.

tube. While there are several very specific options for the results of this operation, essentially (just like the **revolve**) the surface is being generated by a loft. The profile curve is being duplicated and moved along the path curve, after which the loft will happen between all the duplicated curves. The resulting surface will have as many spans as the profile curve has. Figure 3.37 shows the profile and path curve, while Figure 3.38 shows the resulting extruded surface. Figure 3.39 illustrates what is really happening when you create the extruded surface—the profile curve is duplicated and moved along the path curve (one for each span), and then they are all lofted together to form the surface. See how every surface creation tool is simply an automated version of a complex loft? It so much easier to use extrude, though, than to waste all that time duplicating and transforming the curves.

Birail, while a much more complex method of generating a surface, deserves mention because it is a unique way of generating a surface. Similar to an extrude, a birail uses a **profile** curve and a **path** curve. However, in this case, there are two path curves and infinite amounts of profile curves. This allows you to create a very complex shape along two "rails" (hence the name), which changes as it lofts itself along from one shape curve to another. Since birail is such a complex tool, it generally requires a lot of pre-planning and specific objective needs in order to use it properly. One of the most important things to understand about creating the birail surface is that the curves must be connected to one another, which

FIGURE 3.38 An extrude surface is made just like squeezing Play-Doh® or pasta through a cutout shape.

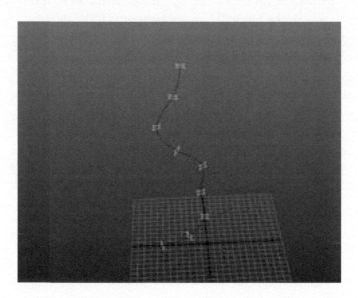

FIGURE 3.39 Under the hood, this is what is really happening. The profile curve is duplicated, positioned along the path curve, and the loft is made between them all.

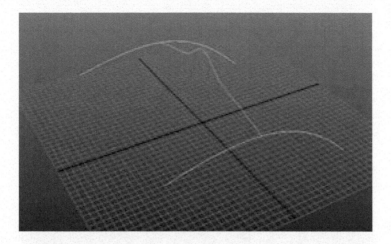

FIGURE 3.40   Two rail curves and one profile curve, with the profile touching the rails on the ends—this is a birail 1.

is accomplished by making sure that the beginning and end CVs of the curve are snapped to the rail curves, which most programs offering this type of surface will have a way to do. C is the hotkey for the curve snap tool in Maya, which will make any object (including sub-objects like the CV) "ride" along the curve rail like a roller coaster. Figure 3.40 is an example of a birail preparation with two rail curves on either side, and a profile curve in the center (notice how the ends are all touching). Figure 3.41 shows the birail surface generated. Birails can have as many profile curves as you want, which allows a staggering amount of control over the surface contour before creating it. Designs for car bodies are a good example of a practical application of this tool. Figures 3.42 and 3.43 show a birail 3-tool setup and completion, in which there are 3 profile curves and 2 rail curves.

Boundary surfaces are surfaces that are created by choosing three or four curves that are connected by their start and end knots. As you can see in Figure 3.45, this allows a surface to be generated by choosing the outline curves. Like the birail, the outline curves must be connected by having the start or end knots in the exact same location, something that can be accomplished by using the **curve snap.** Figure 3.44 shows four curves with the corners that are connected together, like a postage stamp. Figure 3.45 shows a boundary surface created from these four curves.

FIGURE 3.41   The resulting birail 1 surface.

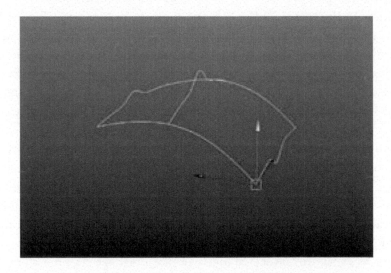

FIGURE 3.42   All the profile curves are lined up along the rail curves.

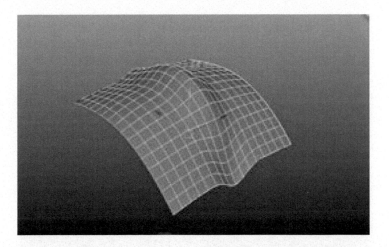

FIGURE 3.43   See how the birail 3 allows the profile to change shape over the length of the rails. It would be very hard to do this with precision just by moving the point around!

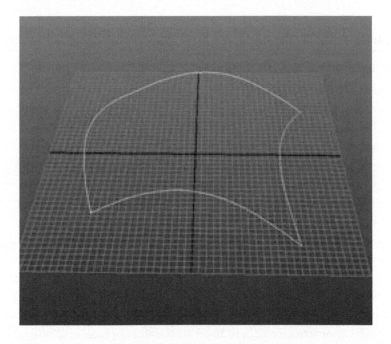

FIGURE 3.44   Four separate curves, intersecting at the end points.

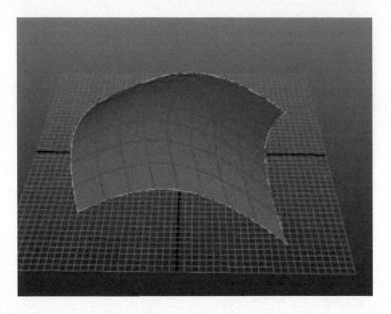

FIGURE 3.45   The resulting boundary surface, made from the intersecting curves.

IS THERE A WAY TO CUT A HOLE IN A NURBS SURFACE?

Projected Curves and Trim Surfaces

Although NURBS surfaces thus far have been pretty useful and shown to build complex surfaces fairly easily, there are a few things that are difficult to do. Unlike polygons, with their face extrusions, NURBS have a really hard time having branching geometry; there is only so much you can do with a ribbon, even if you can adjust it in a dozen ways with its U and V curves. What about at least putting a hole in the surface? What about extending a surface from a surface? **Projected curves** and **trim** surfaces allow us to accomplish these otherwise difficult tasks.

Projecting a curve is taking a NURBS curve and making a duplicate of it that conforms to the shape of the surface. This is accomplished by using the U and V elements of the surface to contour the curve to the shape. Because every NURBS surface is essentially a flat ribbon, we can take any curve and "stick" it to that surface. After doing so, the "projected" curve will automatically adhere itself to the 2D surface, and will only be able to move in the NURBS surface U and V (it will no longer have three axes of movement). Figure 3.46 shows a NURBS curve that has been projected onto a NURBS surface, and the resulting curve-on-surface has been

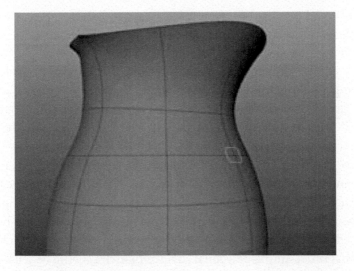

FIGURE 3.46 The projected curve, which is highlighted, is conforming to the shape of the surface.

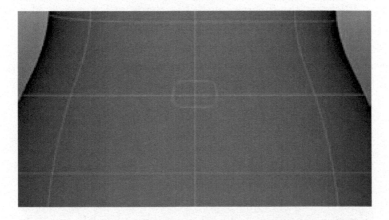

FIGURE 3.47 Because the NURBS surface is just a flat ribbon, it can be laid out in 2D with a U and V direction.

highlighted. Notice that there are now two curves—the original 3D curve and the new 2D curve, which can only move along the surface. The 2D, or projected curve, retains its shape from the original curve because of history, but it also continuously conforms to the surface on which it has been projected. This is because the curve is actually being calculated on the U and V of the surface in two dimensions, as you can see in Figure 3.47. Every NURBS surface is just a flat plane that has been wrapped around curves like wires, and because of this, it is very easy to adhere a projected curve to the shape of the surface. The curve will maintain the surface contour if the surface is changed.

What can we do with this curve now that it has been projected? The first thing we do is use it to create a **trim**. In order to create a trim, we need a closed or periodic curve. You can see how generating a trim surface will "cut" a hole in that surface in the exact shape of the curve. Alternatively, you can create a surface with just the projected curve, which will leave you with a surface in the shape of the projected curve, with the same contours of the surface. Think of this like a donut—you can have either the donut or the donut hole. We have a use for both. This, incidentally, is the only way that we can create a surface that does not have square edges! Mathematically what is happening when you trim the surface is that the resulting polygonal surface (which is being tessellated) will approximate the shape of the cutout with as many polygons as necessary to generate the smoothed curve. Figure 3.48 shows the projected curve from Figure 3.47 after it has been turned into a hole with a NURBS trim. Figure 3.49 shows the inverse—only the shape of the projected curve is preserved and the rest has been trimmed away. When you create a trim surface, you create a new sub-object called a **trim edge.** A trim edge is the place where the projected curve was turned into a trim surface. You can see in Figure 3.50 the resulting trim edge (which is the same whether you

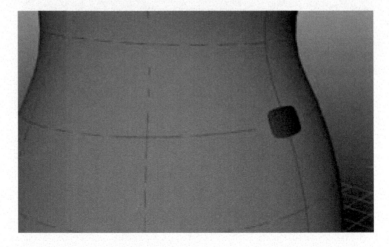

FIGURE 3.48 The trim being made. This trim kept the object and put a hole where the projected curve was.

FIGURE 3.49 The hole kept and the object trimmed.

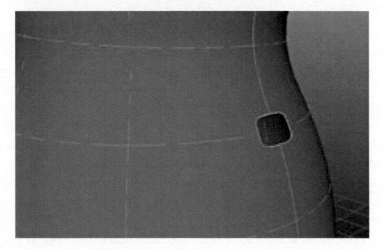

FIGURE 3.50 The resulting trim edge.

cut the hole or cut out the hole). You can select that sub-object and perform surface creation actions to it (see next in the following paragraph on fillets). You can continue the trim process with as many as you want, but the process gets more complex each time you run it and heavily trimmed surfaces can become slow when processing. This is often the case when building a surface with a lot of precision detail for engineering, which is one reason why they require a lot of computing power.

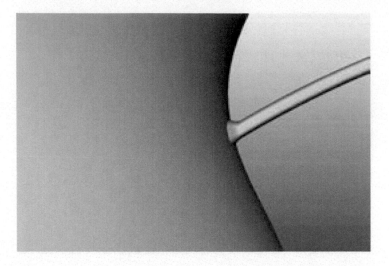

FIGURE 3.51 Two surfaces, one "extruding" from the other by using projected curves.

The second reason for using a projected curve on surface is for creating branching geometry. While there can be no true branching of NURBS geometry like you can do with polygonal geometry, you can create multiple surfaces with seamless transitions that provide the illusion of branching geometry. This is important because it is the only way you will be able to make a branching model using only NURBS. A surface is generated from a curve that has been projected onto another surface. When the second surface is created, it will appear as if the two surfaces are smoothly branched or connected. Figure 3.51 shows a NURBS surface that has been connected between one surface and another, appearing to be branching out from it. There is a pitcher, which has had a handle extended from the top portion. There are actually three surfaces here: the original pitcher, the intermediate surface, and the handle surface. The handle was extruded from a copy of the curve that was projected onto the pitcher surface, and the intermediate surface was lofted between them. Figure 3.52 shows the duplicated surface curve, and Figure 3.53 shows the extruded handle surface. Figure 3.54 shows the intermediate surface, which is generated by lofting together the curve on the surface and the profile curve of the extrusion. The intermediate surface was slightly tweaked in order to create the smoothed transition from the surface of the pitcher to the extruded tubular handle.

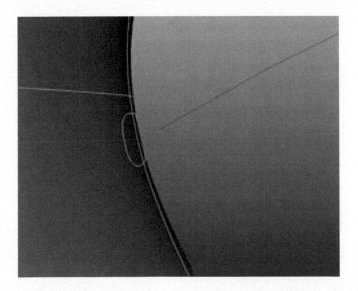

FIGURE 3.52 A curve in the surface is used to create a tube extrusion along a path.

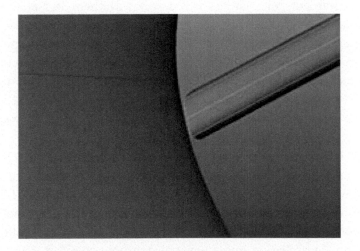

FIGURE 3.53 The resulting tube-extruded surface.

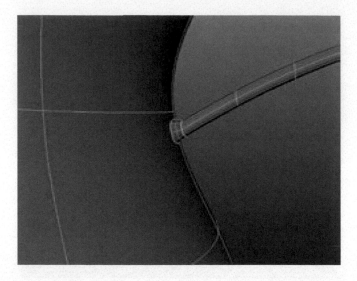

FIGURE 3.54   A third surface is created to transition between the two surfaces in order to appear seamless.

HOW DO I CONVERT NURBS INTO POLYGONS?

While polygon models are not immediately convertible into NURBS models, the opposite is quite a different story. Remember what we learned earlier about NURBS and tessellation? NURBS surfaces are constantly being converted into polygon triangles as you work with them. In fact, they have to in order to be displayed on the screen (see the rendering section). So, converting a NURBS model into polygons is actually very simple—it is already being done for you all the time! Most programs allow you to make a one-time conversion when you want to generate a polygonal model from your curve-based one. The hardest thing to determine is how detailed you want the resulting model to be and what mode of conversion you want to use.

There is a dizzying array of options when converting your NURBS surface to polygons, but the real question is whether you want a uniform conversion or an adaptive one. Remember that NURBS surfaces are descriptions of areas that are constantly being converted into polygons. When you are converting a surface to a polygon, you are just solidifying that adaptive tessellation into a new polygon-only object. It is important to know what you are planning to do with the object after conversion if

FIGURE 3.55 The pitcher on the left is NURBS and the pitcher on the right is polygons, uniformly converted with one edge loop per span in the U and V. Notice how much smoother the NURBS pitcher is.

you want to have a good guideline for what options to use. The nice thing about the history feature is that you can keep creating new versions of your converted surface by tweaking the settings and see it update in real time.

Uniform polygon tessellation uses the spans of the NURBS surface to generate the polygons. Each CV of the surface you are converting will generate a polygon vertex, which also means that each hull of the surface will create an edge loop. This is by far the most common way to convert simple NURBS objects such as our water pitcher. In Figure 3.55, you can see the pitcher converted using a uniform method. You can increase or decrease the amount of edge loops generated by the conversion in both the U and V, giving you a good deal of flexibility in how detailed or simple you want the polygon version to appear. Figure 3.56 shows you the same conversion, but this time the settings have been turned up to create three edge loops for every one span in the U and V. Uniform conversion is great for objects on which you intend to do texture coordinates and possibly deform for character animation. It also works well for simple objects like this pitcher, which can benefit from having uniform spacing for all of the polygon edge loops.

Adaptive tessellation is uneven. It uses a series of equations to find the areas where you need more polygons to make certain areas of your object

FIGURE 3.56   The amount of edge loops generated has been increased to three per NURBS span in the U and V.

smoother, and it uses fewer polygons where you need less. The advantage to this is that it can reduce the overall polygon count, but the disadvantage is that the result will be completely uneven, and in many cases create bad topology and split faces when using quad polygons (as opposed to triangles). The place that adaptive tessellation is important is when you have trim surfaces. Trim surfaces require far more polygons in the area of the trim than they do in other areas of the surface, making it important to subdivide the trim area heavily while leaving the rest of the object less detailed. In Figure 3.57, you can see the trim hole on the pitcher as it appears when converted to polygons using a uniform type of conversion setting. You can see how jagged the trim hole is. If we wanted the trim hole to be very smooth and everything to be uniform, we would have to subdivide the object so many times it would be incredibly dense, as you can see in Figure 3.58. Figure 3.59 shows the solution to this problem; by adaptively converting the polygons you can see that the faces are subdivided more in the trim area than in the rest of the object, which saves over 3000 polygons while keeping the trim hole just as smooth.

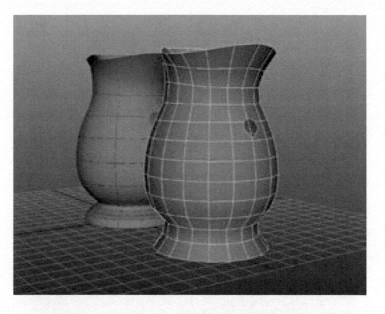

FIGURE 3.57 Uniformly converted, but the trim hole is very jagged!

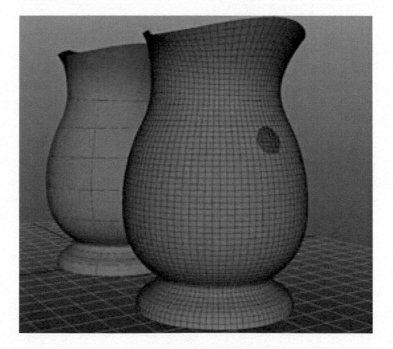

FIGURE 3.58 We can turn up the amount of subdivisions, but now we have way more polygons than we need.

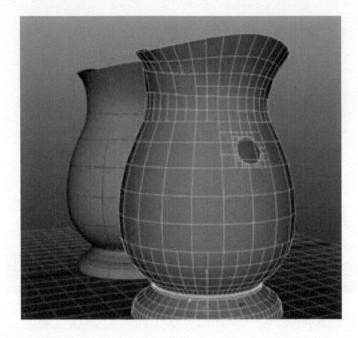

FIGURE 3.59 Adaptive conversion.

NURBS CONCEPTS CONCLUSION— WHEN DO I USE NURBS?

NURBS is one method of modeling among many. In this chapter, you have learned the basic underpinnings of the curve-based system of modeling. There are clear advantages to this style of modeling, and clear disadvantages. One of the greatest things about NURBS and curve-based modeling is that it can be extremely accurate, which makes it a great tool for modeling things that will have to become real-world objects, like bicycle seats, airplane wings, and even iPhone cases you print out on a 3D printer. Another advantage to NURBS is that it can be constantly tessellated during render times, which makes it important for film output, and companies such as Pixar have long used NURBS in production due to their ability to always be smooth at high resolutions no matter how close the camera gets to them. On the other hand, NURBS can be very difficult to model with, and the rules of the surface are not very flexible in creating detail only in specific areas, which leaves the other areas with less. Polygons are best suited for this, as well as for creating branching geometry for organic surfaces such as arms and legs, fingers, antennae, and all other extrusions from a branch. Knowing when to model with what technique is often a result of experience and knowing the intended output. When you are first starting out, it will seem challenging just trying to figure out what type of modeling you will choose. Generally, the best advice is to give it some thought before you decide, and look over your options. Some universal rules can apply. NURBS is great for inanimate objects, while polygons are good for organic models. There is no reason that you cannot create any model with either of these two methods, however, and the most important thing to keep in mind as a modeler is that your skill, experience, and ability will make the most difference in the end.

EXERCISE: THE WINE GLASS

This quick tutorial is a great way to understand several aspects of NURBS curves and surface generation. We are going to create a wine glass out of NURBS.

Step 1: Creating the Profile Curve

Make sure that you are in the "surfaces" module, which you can locate on the upper left-hand menu. One of the best things about NURBS and curve-based modeling is that we can define the shape of a surface by the curve in the simplest form possible. The first thing we are going to do is create a curve that defines the shape of the wine glass. Go to the front orthographic view and choose Create > CV Curve, using the linear option for type. We use linear curves when creating a CV curve because it is far easier to envision the final shape when doing it in a linear manner. You can also easily use the grid snap option to make sure that the CV curves you draw are aligned nicely. Draw the outline of the wine glass, to the left of the central Y-axis, as in Figure 3.61.

Step 2: Re-Building the Curve

Once you have successfully created the curve, you will need to re-build it using the Rebuild Curve action. This will allow you to convert it into a cubic, or smooth curve. This step makes it easy to take any curve and re-build it with a dizzying array of parameters—the procedural control over NURBS curve and surfaces is their best feature! Select your curve, open the Edit Curve > Rebuild Curve option box, and choose the options as shown in Figure 3.62. This will rebuild your curve as a smooth curve with the same amount of CV points. The curve will now be cubic, or drawn with smooth lines instead of straight ones, as it appears in Figure 3.63.

FIGURE 3.60   Options to create a CV curve.

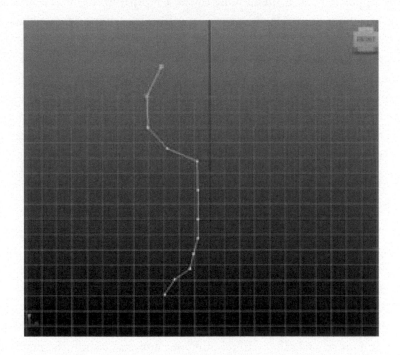

FIGURE 3.61   Linear curve drawn in the shape of a wine glass.

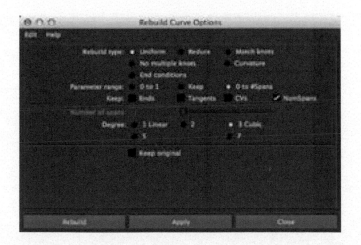

FIGURE 3.62 There are many options, but make sure that Keep: NumSpans is selected and Degree: Cubic is checked!

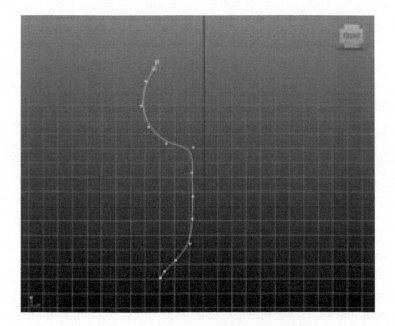

FIGURE 3.63 The linear curve is now smooth (or cubic).

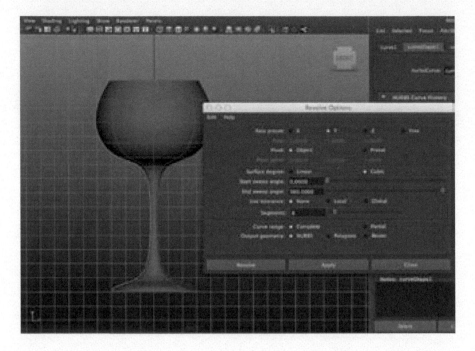

FIGURE 3.64 The revolve surface options and the resulting wine glass surface created.

Step 3: Creating the Surface

OK, now that we have a curve that nicely defines the shape of our wine glass from the front, we are going to generate the surface from it. Remember that the surface is always generated from some form of loft operation, which creates a "skin" between two or more curves. In this case, we are going to use the Surfaces > Revolve Surface Action, which will generate a NURBS surface by duplicating your profile curve several times, rotating that curve around an axis, and then lofting them all together to form a closed surface, or "skin." Sometimes this action is called a "lathe" because of its similarity to a lathe saw. Notice how the surface now looks just like your profile. Because of the construction history aspect of Maya, you can edit the original curve and you will see the entire surface update as a result.

Congratulations! In a few simple steps, you have created a nicely modeled NURBS wine glass. Notice how the surface has no depth. One of the things we have learned about NURBS is that it cannot have depth at all; making it more like a "skin" or a canvas stretched over a set of wires that define its shape.

CHAPTER 4

Lighting, Materials, Textures, and UVs

WHAT IS "RENDERING"?

You will often hear the term "rendering" in connection to 3D computer graphics. It is tossed around a lot, often without any real subjective explanation. After a while (say, 10 years), you start to get what rendering is, but you might be embarrassed that you can't clearly define it in dictionary-like terms. **Rendering** is the act of converting any geometry (2D or 3D) into pixels on your screen or saved in an image file. Although this sounds incredibly simple, the calculations needed to perform this operation are incredibly complex, and have been in the process of development for almost 50 years. It takes many calculations just to make a single pixel appear on your screen based on geometry in a 2D or 3D computer graphics package.

The important thing to understand first, in terms of 3D geometry and rendering, is that the stuff you see on your screen isn't really the same thing as the geometry. It is the visual representation of math stuff going on underneath the hood. Your surfaces and polygons exist without pixels—they are all just plotted points in space and mathematical equations. There are no pixels associated with them in their raw state, just a bunch of numbers in a format based on a Cartesian grid. It is important to remember that because if you do, you will start to peel back the mystical connection between what you see on your screen and what the computer sees. In Figure 4.1, you can see the text description of a sphere in Maya. In Figure 4.2, you can see that sphere appear on your screen.

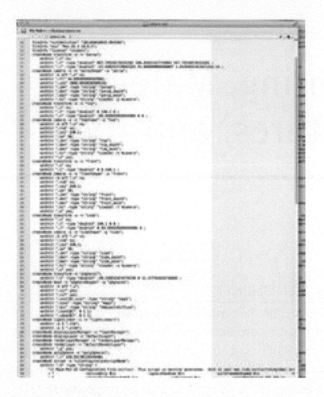

FIGURE 4.1   3D is mostly numbers.

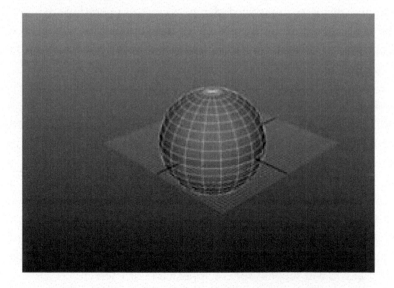

FIGURE 4.2   Those numbers converted into an image on the screen.

So how does this stuff get to the screen? Well, that is where rendering comes into play. Unless you are some kind of mathematical genius who can see grid numbers in 3D space in your head, you will need some visual method of making sense of all these plotted points for geometry. That is where the rendering "engine" comes into play. It is called an engine because it does a lot of work. It draws lines between those points in space (as NURBS curves or polygon edges) and shows them to you by calculating pixels to the monitor in RGB data. It also fills in all those spaces in between the lines, which are being calculated as triangles, with pixels too. This is why we can see a 3D image that seems to have depth and volume—we call this **shading**, and we will talk about it in detail later.

GPU vs. CPU Rendering

Now that we know what rendering is and how the computer calculates all of those points in space to pixels, we need to understand a little bit about where those pixels are going. In the previous example, I used the screen as the depository of that information, so let's start with that. When your computer calculates pixels and displays them to your screen, it is doing so on the fly, or as you are looking at it. This is called "real-time" graphics, and it is generally handled on the graphics processing unit (GPU). This is the processor on your video card, which is highly tuned to do the necessary calculations for turning 3D information into pixels, which then feed a video signal to your monitor. The GPU has to calculate this at 60 Hz, or 60 images per second, because it has to keep up with what you are doing in the software. Every time you move the camera around and look at an object it will change what you are seeing, which is happening at a very fast rate. This is also what is happening when you play a game on a PC or console. The game is calculating everything in real-time because you as the player are making changes to the view, pressing buttons to control the character, and seeing updates on your Heads Up Display. All of this is being rendered by your GPU, and very quickly. For this reason, the GPU can only handle a limited amount of calculations at a time. Too much would overwhelm it or slow it down to a crawl. This is why real-time graphics never look as good as movies—although this will change in the years to come as GPUs get faster and smarter. However, as it stands, the GPU is geared more for speed than quality because you would always prefer better interaction than quality when playing a game or working with a 3D program. So those

FIGURE 4.3 **(SEE COLOR INSERT)** Real-time rendering of a game in development by the author.

pixels are being calculated lightning fast in order to allow you to interact with the 3D world you are developing.

There are specific calculations in specific mathematical models or APIs that are designed to handle all of this information quickly. The two current popular models are OpenGL and Direct3D by Microsoft. You don't need to know extremely detailed facts about these APIs; however, it is nice to understand that these are the predetermined calculations that are set up to deliver the pixels to your graphics card so you can see the 3D objects.

The second type of rendering is known as **software rendering**. It occurs mainly on the central processing unit (CPU) inside your computer. This is when you take all of the lighting, shadows, extra material options, textures, and filters and calculate them into a single bitmap image (like a tif or jpg file). Software rendering takes a lot longer than real-time rendering (sometimes hours per individual frame), but it can produce amazingly rich, realistic results. Look at Figure 4.4 and see the amazing amount of realism and depth. This could never happen in real-time because the calculations would simply take too long. However, when we render to images we are not trying to make it interactive, we are trying to get the best possible result we can in either a single still image or a sequence of images, which we would then turn into a film or video. Software rendering is known to take so long that there are giant rendering farms at big CG studios, multiple computers in banks, crunching away at multiple frames for playback as the movie develops. It takes a lot of memory as well to render high-resolution images.

FIGURE 4.4 **(SEE COLOR INSERT)** Software rendering. Notice the high quality of this render. It could never be achieved at 60 frames per second (fps) with today's hardware.

WHAT ARE THE THINGS REQUIRED TO RENDER A SCENE?

Lights, Camera, Materials!

Rendering is not a simple process. Every 3D scene, regardless of the software package, must have certain items in it in order to generate pixels. It is important to understand how each of them affects the resulting image in either real-time or software rendering. Following is a list of the necessary components for rendering any 3D object and scene. We will explore all of these items in depth later in the chapter.

1. **Geometry**—It would seem obvious, but sometimes it is important to realize that there is only one thing that can be rendered in a 3D scene, and that is 3D geometry. All of the following items are specifically designed to perform the rendering operation.

2. **Cameras**—Cameras are just what they say they are—projection cameras that mimic the perspective of the human eye or a movie camera. A camera is necessary to produce the visual aspect of the geometry in order to render it into pixels. It creates the parallax and perspective that gives the 3D look to objects. Although the camera is necessary in order for us to *see* the geometry in a scene, it does not mean

that it does not exist without us seeing it. It is the old, "If a tree falls in a forest and nobody is there to hear it fall, does it make a sound?" In this case, the question is, "If there is no camera in a 3D scene with which we can preview the geometry, is the geometry really there?" In this case, the answer is absolutely yes! The geometry exists as mathematical data, regardless if there is a camera in the scene. It is not that valuable to us if we cannot see it, but it is important to understand that it would still be there, as data, even if the camera were not. Cameras generally have aspects to them that mimic real world cameras—focal length, field of view, depth of field, etc. We will study the camera attributes that are common to all software programs.

3. **Lights**—Lights are how a scene is "illuminated." Without any lights in a scene, everything would appear to be dark. Light bounces off the geometry, using the **normal** information of the vertices to calculate the **shading**, which generates light and dark information about the pixels being rendered. Most 3D programs have default lights set up so that when interacting with the software and test rendering you can see the objects in question. However, when you create your own lights those default lights are turned off. This is confusing to most people when they first start using a 3D program because it is never made clear that without any lights at all, the scene would be dark. We will spend a lot of time on lights and lighting in the next section because they are so important in making a 3D scene look appealing.

4. **Shaders**—Shaders are mathematical calculations that take the information from the lights and apply it in certain ways to the 3D object, which is ultimately broken down into polygonal triangles in order to create pixels from the lighting information. Shaders are important because they provide the basis for what kind of calculation will occur—shiny, known as **specular** or non-shiny (**non-specular**). There are many different shaders used in various software packages, but the most common non-specular shaders are called **Lambert**, and the most common **specular** shaders are known as **Blinn**, **Phong**, and **Anisotropic**.

5. **Materials**—Materials are how color, texture, and all other information are prepared for a rendering pipeline. Materials first use one type of shader, which determines which attributes are available. This is true across the board in terms of applications, even game

middleware such as Unreal and Unity, which have a much more optimized material pipeline for real-time than animation production material editors, such as 3D Studio Max or Maya. When you choose what shader you will be using for a material, it will determine what options are available for you to edit. In production software geared a little more toward software rendering, you will get a lot more options for a standard material, whereas in programs such as Unity or Unreal, you will get extremely limited options that help streamline the process for resource conservation. Materials are several **channels**, which are combined together in the rendering pipeline (real-time or software) in order to generate the pixels that will make up the final rendered image.

HOW DO CAMERAS WORK IN 3D?

Cameras and Camera Attributes

When setting up a 3D scene to render, it is necessary to understand through what perspective you are rendering your scene. Since the camera tends to be an "invisible" object, most learning users tend to ignore it or not be aware of its presence. When modeling, you are constantly looking through the camera without realizing that it is there, and when it comes to setting up a scene for rendering the tendency is to overlook the vital job of setting up a specific camera for rendering the scene.

Cameras are like cameras in real life. They have similar properties and those properties can be adjusted. The most important thing to understand when dealing with cameras is **parallax**. Parallax is the visual effect of converging lines. When you are looking through a **perspective** camera, the scene is displayed as you see it in the real world. That is, objects that are further away from you are smaller than ones that are closer to you. Figure 4.5 illustrates this effect with two identical spheres. One of them is further away on the Z-axis than the other one. Because of the difference in distance, the one further away looks smaller. Perspective cameras are usually used to render scene into images for animation, and they represent film cameras or our own eyes. The other kind of camera is called **orthographic**. This is when all of the objects in a scene are seen from a flat point of view, in which distance from the camera does not change the size of the object in the viewport. Generally, orthographic cameras are for modeling and object layout or alignment. Figure 4.6 illustrates the view of

FIGURE 4.5 The sphere on the right is smaller because it is further away from the camera. This is known as parallax.

FIGURE 4.6 This is an orthographic view of the same scene, but because it lacks parallax the spheres are the same size.

the same two spheres, but this time in a front orthographic view. Notice that the spheres are the same size in the viewport, despite one of them being very further away from the camera.

Camera attributes will drastically change the way the objects and scene are drawn in the viewport. Because of the necessity for calculations similar to the real world, there are certain attributes that are universal for the cameras to function, which are accessible in all 3D programs. These attributes with their respective descriptions are listed here.

Focal Length—The focal length refers the length of the lens, which in turn affects the angle of view. This will change how much you can fit into your camera's view. For instance, a wide, panoramic-style shot would require a much smaller focal length but cause major distortion around the edges (of a convex nature). A much tighter shot would require a much bigger focal length but would also have distortion of a concave nature around the edges of the shot (also known as a "fish-eye" lens). In the real world, you would have to change lenses on the camera, but in 3D, we can simply dial it higher or lower as needed. The standard, and default in many 3D packages, is 35 millimeters, which is closest to the human eye. Any custom changes in this and you will be able to create some interesting shots, but you may want to take at least a crash course in cinematography or traditional photography first.

Clipping Planes—This is always a concern when creating 3D content because there has to be a point at which the camera decides not to display or render something. There is always a near and a far clipping plane, and these clipping planes determine when the camera ceases to draw to the screen. If you are working with very small objects in the viewport, like individual vertices, sometimes you will have to

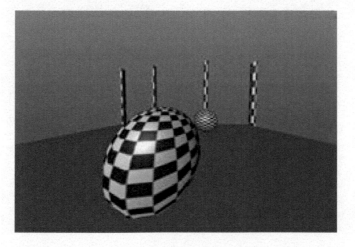

FIGURE 4.7 Small focal length and a fish-eye appearance as the closer objects appear distorted.

FIGURE 4.8 Large focal length and the scene becomes less angular and more orthographic, with relative distance being harder to see.

move the near clipping plane closer to the camera in order to zoom in on them. The opposite goes for objects very far away from the camera. Objects that are distant could cease to draw if they are further from the camera than the clipping plane. Figure 4.9 illustrates a camera in 3D with a near and far clipping plane. Only objects inside the two planes (representing near and far clipping planes) will be rendered by the camera.

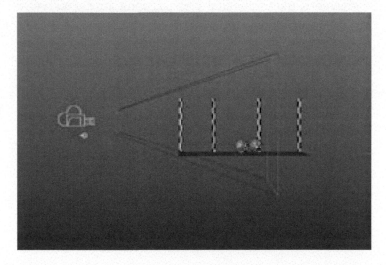

FIGURE 4.9 Clipping planes tell the camera where to render and where not to render objects.

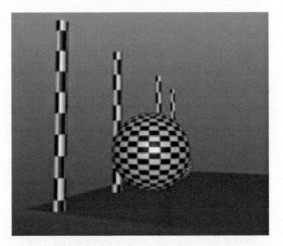

FIGURE 4.10 Objects further away are blurry when the depth of field is turned on.

Depth of Field—Depth of field is a phenomenon that focuses the camera on a single point in space, making the objects grow more blurry as they get further from the point in focus or if they are closer to the camera. This is the same effect as looking through the windshield of your car when a bug splatters onto it—looking at the bug, which is just a couple of feet from your face, causes the cars in the distance to get blurry. The same thing occurs when you look back to traffic and the bug on the windshield gets blurry while the objects far away come into focus. You can mimic this effect at render time with the depth of field setting, which is altered from the focal point setting, which sets the point at which the camera is fully focused. Figure 4.10 shows the effect of setting a depth of field focal point for a render.

WHAT IS SHADING?

The Polygon Normal

Shading and **shader** are words that you will hear in conjunction with 3D graphics a lot, but rarely will a 3D artist be able to clearly define what a shader is and what it does. A shader breaks down the geometry, lighting, and camera information in the scene and applies the appropriate level of light, dark, and color pixels to the rendering pipeline. It is a mathematical formula that converts the rendering items (camera, lights, and **polygon normal** information) into pixels based on attributes or channels that calculate what color each pixel should be. There are many different kinds of shaders, and there are ways to write custom shading equations for special information and effects.

The first important element that controls shading is the polygon normal. The normal is a sub-object of the polygon of sorts, in that it is selectable and editable, but it is separate from the vertex, edge, and face in that it is derived or calculated from the angle of the face. This is important because it does not control the shape of the polygon; rather, the shape of the polygon controls it.

The first type of normal for us to look at is the **face normal**. The face normal is the perpendicular angle of the polygon face. In Figure 4.11, you can see a single polygon triangle in perspective with the normal showing. The normal, as you can see, looks like a hair sticking straight out of the polygon face. Since the triangle is always planar (flat), you can always calculate the 90-degree angle from its flat face. When dealing with a quad, or multi-sided polygon, the normal of that face will be an average of all the triangles of which it consists. You can see in Figure 4.12 that the non-planar polygon with two triangle has two normals, but when it is displayed as a quad in Figure 4.13 it only has a single normal, averaged from the values of the two implied triangles. It is notable to remember that you can move a polygon face along the normal in most software packages. This allows you to move geometry based on the way it is already facing, instead of trying to move it based on the world or local coordinates, and allows a great deal of flexibility with organic shapes, which are rarely aligned with the world axis.

FIGURE 4.11   A single polygon triangle with the face normal showing.

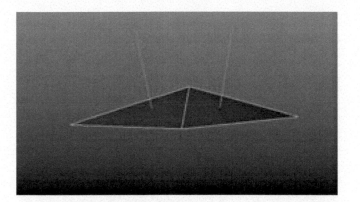

FIGURE 4.12   A quad divided into two triangles with each possessing its own face normal.

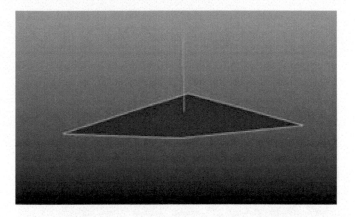

FIGURE 4.13   A quad without triangulation showing a single combined face normal, which is averaged from the two triangular face normals.

A **vertex normal** is the second type of normal. It is derived from the face normal. Now here is where it gets confusing—you can have more than one normal per vertex! In fact, the basic normal configuration without any **smoothing** (more on that later) is to have a normal for each face to which the vertex is attached. You can see in Figure 4.14 that this vertex, part of a polygon sphere, has a normal for each face to which it is attached, giving it four total normals. Each of those normals has the exact same angle as the face with which they are associated.

Most software packages, and the standard setup for primitive objects, is to have the vertex normal **smoothed** where the surface is round. This means that all four normals from Figure 4.15 will be combined, each one

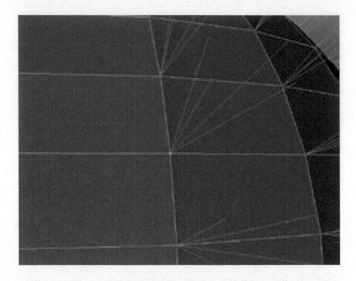

FIGURE 4.14   When normals have been set on a per-face basis, there is a single vertex normal for every face connected to it.

FIGURE 4.15   Normals that are averaged have only one per vertex.

averaged together to make a single value. This is most common in smooth objects, like the sphere we are looking at. In Figure 4.16, we can see the same vertex, with combined normal so that the flow of angles from normal to normal is consistent. This is necessary for the image to appear as if it is smooth because if all the normal were split, you would see this object as it would appear in the real world, which is just a bunch of flat planes

FIGURE 4.16   A faceted appearance is the result of having a single normal per face.

FIGURE 4.17   This is the same geometry, but with normals averaged.

welded together. Figure 4.17 shows how a sphere appears when all of the normals are set to the individual vertices. Notice how it looks like a bunch of flat squares that have been glued together. This is what it looks like when the shading is not smoothed across the vertices by averaging the normal and combining them into a single value.

FIGURE 4.18   A simple scene setup to learn lighting and light properties.

So the real question, you might be asking yourself, is what do the normals have to do with shading? The answer is everything. The normal creates angles from which the lights in the scene strike the object. The light rays hit the vertex normal and the vertex is told to be rendered a certain way with certain color pixels, which is in turn based on the angle of that particular vertex to the angle of the light rays. When a light ray hits the normal, it will give a brightness value based on a range between 180 degrees (light is directly striking it and brightness is 100%), or 90 degrees (light is perpendicular and brightness is at 0%). Without that normal information, lighting and shading could not be calculated. The shader tells the rendering pipeline what pixels to put to the screen or still image based on the information in the normals and the lighting. Those pixels will be lighter or darker, depending on the angle of the light. As the light moves across the surface, it renders darker and darker pixels when the angles of the normal reach 90 degrees. This creates a smooth transition from bright to dark area, and this process is known as shading. You can see in Figures 4.16 and 4.17 how the difference between smoothing the normal changes the appearance of the sphere significantly.

WHAT ARE LIGHTS?

Lights and Lighting

Lighting is one of those aspects of 3D that is so large it is hard to tackle in conceptual, beginner terms. The most important thing to understand about lights is that they are responsible for creating brightness in the scene—without any lights, there would be nothing to render. Lights are set up to provide a more realistic 3D appearance to your models. Without changes in light, dark, and shadow, your objects would not appear to be 3D at all (even though they still would be 3D data). One confusing thing when working in 3D is that most software packages have auto-lighting enabled, which uses a standard 3-light setup to preview your objects in the modeling view. Without these auto-lights, you would have nothing to see. Usually these auto lights are killed when an actual light is created.

There are four traditional, core types of lights: ambient, directional, point, and spot. Many more types have been in use for years (global illumination, area lights, etc.) but they are generally specialized to high-level realistic lighting simulations that are outside the scope of this book. We want to deal with the old-school lights because not only are they the most commonly used but they are the only kind used in real-time gaming platforms. Real-time (GPU) lighting cannot calculate the super-realistic lighting models that rendered images can take advantage of. Someday perhaps they will, but for now, we want to stick to the basics.

Types of Lights

Ambient Light

The ambient light is the simplest of lights. It casts light everywhere all at once, from every direction. Ambient lighting does not produce areas of light and shadow because it does not come from a direction. It is best used for brightening up or tinting a scene globally. Some game systems use **pre-lighting**, or baking the light information into the textures that are on the geometry. In this case, the ambient light alone works well and saves valuable calculation time. In Figure 4.19, you can see two spheres being lit with an ambient light. It is very washed out and lacks a 3D appearance. This is because there is no change of lighting across the surface at all. The light casts in all angles to all vertex normals at once, which makes the illumination completely even. Ambient lighting can be used to boost natural lighting conditions or to globally brighten a scene without changing the existing light setup.

Directional Light

Directional light casts light in a vector, or direction, infinitely. It means that no matter where the light is in space, the rays are always coming at a certain angle, determined by the rotation of the light node. You can see in

FIGURE 4.19 Two spheres lit by an ambient light. The light is completely even across the surface.

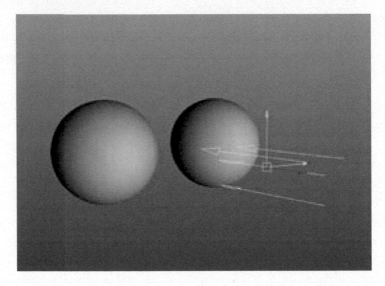

FIGURE 4.20 A directional or parallel light, evenly lighting both spheres.

Figure 4.20, there are two spheres, both being lit by the same directional light (which is in between them). Despite the fact that the light is in front of the sphere to the right of the screen, it is still lit the exact same way as the sphere in front of it. This is because the angle of the light controls how the light affects the object, and not the position of the light. If you rotate the light, however, as you see in Figure 4.21, you will notice that the direction the light is coming from changes (equally for both spheres). A directional light is often used to simulate the Sun because its properties

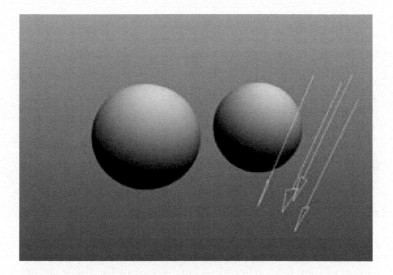

FIGURE 4.21   Changing the angle of the light changes its lighting effect.

are similar, and the time of day can be animated by simply rotating the directional light. For that reason, outdoor scenes are generally lit primarily with a single directional light (although a second helper light is also sometimes employed).

Point Light
A point light is very similar to a light bulb. It is a point in space, which is emanating light in all directions, but only from the point in space. Translating the light will change the affect on the shaded objects (unlike the directional light), but rotating the light will not do anything because it is always casting the light in all directions. You can see in Figure 4.22 there are several images of the spheres being lit by a single point light in different places; unlike the directional light, the point light shines on different parts of the two spheres in the image because the light is being cast from a point in space instead of an angle. Point lights are generally used for open sources of indoor light, such as a light bulbs, candles, or similar objects.

Point lights are the most expensive to calculate in rendering because every angle of light to every polygon normal must be calculated. This is important when trying to create low-imprint scenes in 3D. You have to use your resources wisely, or it will be too much for the rendering system to handle properly. Although the hardware and software capabilities have increased exponentially over the past decade, devices like the iPhone, iPad, and Android do not have the same graphics processing power as a

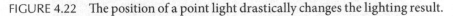

FIGURE 4.22   The position of a point light drastically changes the lighting result.

full computer. Therefore, when developing games for them conservation of resources is still very much an issue. Point lights can often be used to simulate the effect of light coming from a single, naked source, such as a light bulb, match, candle, or lantern. It generally is not a natural light, however, and when trying to create a sunlight or outdoor appearance, it would not be the best light to choose.

Spotlight
A spotlight is exactly what it sounds like. Essentially, a spotlight is a cone of light created by taking a point light and only emanating light from a certain angle, which forms a circular cone. It is very useful for generating the effect of a spotlight, headlight, or flashlight. In Figure 4.23, you can see the spotlight and its effect on the polygon sphere. Spotlights are faster to calculate than point lights because the light rays only need to be calculated as emanating from them at angles inside the radius angle.

Common Light Attributes

All lights share some attributes, and some are unique to the individual type of light. Here is a list of several attributes that can be edited, what they do, and which light uses them.

> **Color**—All light types have this attribute, which determines the RGB value of the color being emitted by the light. This mixes with the shading information and the normal values to produce the pixels on the screen. Most natural light is in the yellow to white spectrum,

FIGURE 4.23 The spotlight shines light in a cone, which you can see the result of on the sphere above.

and most bulb-style light is as well. Florescent can be a tad on the blue range. Despite all of this, it is very noticeable when you change the color of a light, so unless you are deliberately setting up a colored light or need to create a mood it would be a bad idea to change this value from pure white. Stick to pure white when dealing with standard illumination like the sun or indoor lighting. In Figure 4.24, you can see the effect of color on a light. Stick to using this for very specific purposes, and unless the lights in your scene are actually colored when rendering, natural light values of white to slightly blue are better. This affects the shading of vertices by adding light to the pixel values.

Intensity—This is the multiplier for the light, which is part of the entire lighting to pixel equation. It is how bright the light is. Every light uses this attribute.

Decay rate—Decay is how the intensity of the light is reduced as the distance from the light is increased. Although this value is turned off by default, it is a more realistic model of how light actually occurs in the real world. In Figures 4.25 and 4.26 you will see a scene lit by a single point light. In Figure 4.25 the light has no decay, while in

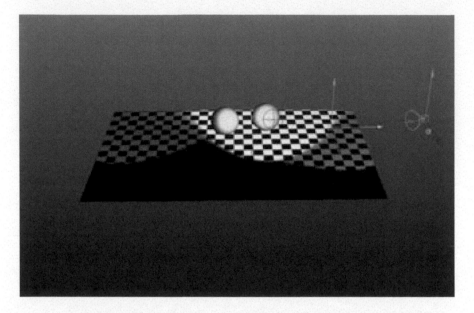

FIGURE 4.24 **(SEE COLOR INSERT)** The effects of using colored lights are very noticeable. Use it sparingly.

FIGURE 4.25 Point light without decay.

Figure 4.26 there is a linear decay rate. You can clearly see that the object further away from the lights grows dimmer, which simulates a real world light, in which the light scatters as it moves away from the source, growing dimmer and dimmer. One thing to note in the decay rate is that the faster the decay rate, the higher the value of

FIGURE 4.26 Point light with decay on. Notice how the closer objects are illuminated more than the further objects. This is what occurs in real life, and is a more realistic model.

intensity will need to be in order for the light to illuminate the area because the light will decay so fast it will not light anything at all. In Figure 4.25 the intensity value is set to 1, yet in Figure 4.26 the intensity value is set to 600. If the value were to be set to 1 in the light using decay, it would appear completely dark because the decay would cause the intensity value of the light to reach zero before it reached the objects. There are several variations on decay speed, and as the rate increases, so will the intensity need to be cranked up in order to see anything in the scene. Decay is only available in lights that emit from a point in space; therefore, only the point light and spotlight can use it.

Spotlight-Specific Parameters

Cone angle—This determines how broad the angle of light will be. A value of 0 will illuminate nothing, while a value of 180 will illuminate everything in a plane, essentially turning a spotlight into a directional light.

Penumbra angle—Penumbra angle is the point at which a spotlight begins to fade out to zero. Without a value here, the spotlight will retain the same brightness across the entire illuminated area.

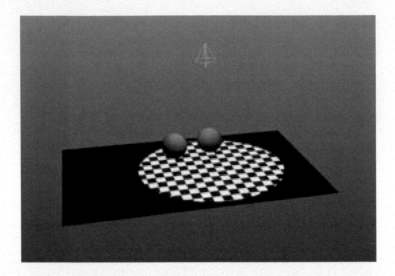

FIGURE 4.27   A spotlight, which emits light in a cone.

FIGURE 4.28   Notice the softening of the edges around the perimeter of the light angle. This is due to the penumbra effect.

Figure 4.27 shows a spotlight hitting an object with no penumbra angle. Figure 4.28 shows the same scene with a penumbra angle of −8 (negative being a value that happens *inside* the radius perimeter, and positive being a value that will occur *after* the perimeter). The penumbra softens the light as it reaches the edges.

Dropoff—This parameter changes the rate of falloff from a light to its perimeter. A high dropoff will fade the light out very quickly and make the edges very diffuse.

Shadows

What is a shadow? Or rather, what isn't a shadow? A shadow, whether in the real world or the simulated world of 3D graphics, is a place where light cannot reach for some reason. Usually that reason is a solid object that is in the way of the light. As the light rays hit the solid object, they do not illuminate the objects behind. The reality of this may be simple, but the physics of this are incredibly complex. While we do not need to comprehend the theory of relativity to understand the concepts of shadows, when you are working with light and trying to understand it, things can get very deep very fast. Luckily, it is not so important to us in what we are trying to achieve when we light a scene in 3D. Our intention is to create a *simulation*, not recreate the physics of the real world and how light travels. There are, in fact, systems that do this (known as radiosity and global illumination), but they are very advanced and beyond the scope of this book. We are here to get a *basic* understanding of 3D concepts and skills. Therefore, we are going to stick to our good, old-fashioned classic light types and tricks to make this work.

Shadows in 3D are calculated in a manner that *simulates* the way they look in the real world, just like the vertex normal and the lights simulate real world lights. In order to make a scene look realistic in any way, the lighting is going to have to look very good, and in order for lighting to work in three dimensions you are going to have to create shadows to give the scene perspective and a sense of parallax. In Figure 4.29, you can see a simple rendered scene without shadows. Notice how the objects touching the ground look odd, awkward, and as if they are floating. In Figure 4.30, you can see that same scene rendered with shadows. Notice how much better it looks? How much more realistic? This is because shadows being rendered do much to recreate the appearance of objects as they would appear in the real world.

There are two kinds of shadows rendered by software programs: **depth map shadows** and **ray-traced shadows**. Each of the shadow types can be changed on a per-light basis, and they are calculated by both the GPU and CPU, although the GPU is extremely limited in this capacity with current technology. Depth map shadows are the cheapest way to calculate

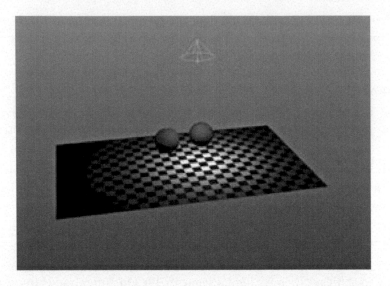

FIGURE 4.29   Notice the softening of the edges around the perimeter of the light angle.

FIGURE 4.30   The greater the dropoff, the faster the intensity of the light value changes to 0.

shadows, in terms of processing power. They are generated by creating renders of the scene from each view of a light in your scene. When the images are rendered, they are then calculated in terms of depth from the light source, and an image file is saved with that depth information. That file is then projected by the light-based view onto the scene with proper depth information, which is converted into pixels to the camera from which you

FIGURE 4.31 Depth map shadows turned on.

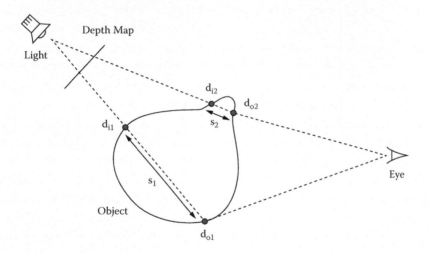

FIGURE 4.32 Did somebody say "math?" Simple explanation of depth maps...

are rendering the scene, and rendered as dark pixels where the light would not fall. If this sounds complex, it is! It is a very complex set of mathematical formulae and conversions being done; however, this is the fastest and most efficient way of generating shadows because only small amounts of information need to be calculated, and the depth maps that are calculated can be constantly re-used as long as the lights stay in the same place. Figure 4.32 is an illustration of the calculations that create the depth map shadows. As you can see, it involves a lot of calculation, but it generally produces decent results.

Depth map shadows have the following limitations:

1. **Cannot calculate semi-transparent objects**—An object's transparency is ignored with depth map shadows because the depth map shadow is just a texture projected onto the screen.

2. **Limited by the resolution**—The resolution of the depth maps must be high enough to match your output render resolution, or you can get very bad aliasing (choppy appearance) around the edges. Turning your depth map resolution can help this, but it eats up memory at render time.

Ray-traced shadows are the second kind of shadows. Ray tracing is a method of rendering that uses straight lines, or "rays," which are calculated through every pixel from the flat plane of the camera and light in the scene. You can see in Figure 4.33 the basic structure of the ray-tracing algorithm in conceptual terms (although the truth is much more "mathy" of course). Ray tracing not only generates shadows because it calculates every line of every light to every object in your scene, but also can produce reflections and refractions with extreme accuracy. For this reason, it is used in high-level rendering to produce very realistic results. The problem with ray tracing is that calculating all of this takes a lot of time, and images are very slow to be rendered, which makes it useless for GPU rendering (at least with the current level of technology). Generally, ray tracing is reserved for software rendering, which is used to produce animations and films in image sequences. Figure 4.34 has an illustration of a scene rendered with ray-traced shadows, while Figure 4.35 shows the

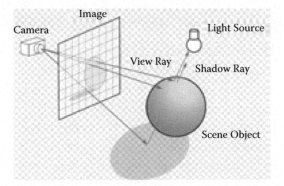

FIGURE 4.33 More math! Ray tracing is slow.

FIGURE 4.34 Depth map shadows produce softer, but less accurate, results.

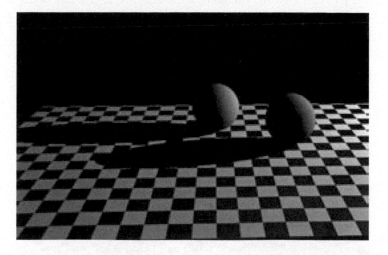

FIGURE 4.35 Ray-traced shadows are slower to render, but produce more accurate results. Also, they are not soft around the edges, which can be unrealistic in less harsh lighting situations.

same scene rendered with depth map shadows. Because the ray-traced shadows are produced by calculating a line through every pixel, they are far more accurate, but the edges of the shadows tend to be crisp, and therefore do not always look natural. Depth map shadows can have a "fuzzy" appearance, which will resemble real-world shadows better because in the real world most shadows are affected by light bouncing off other surfaces (called **radiosity**).

WHEN DO I USE DEPTH MAP SHADOWS?
WHEN DO I USE RAY TRACING?

Choosing Shadow Types

Determining which type of shadow to use is something the new user often asks. However, when setting up a scene for rendering, the answer is usually very subjective to the look you are trying to achieve and the desired realism of the final product. Software rendering is very time-consuming and requires a lot of planning to create a realistic scene with realistic lighting. The simplest rule in any 3D production work is to start with the simplest and cheapest solution (in this case, depth map shadows) and if that is not sufficient, then layer on more complex solutions. If you can get away with the simplest solution, then it works much better than over-thinking or over-complicating things. When a totally photo-real lighting solution is *necessary,* you can look for the complex solutions. If you just want to render a ball bouncing on a floor, then why over-do it? I often feel that I cannot get the ideal appearance by using just one type of shadow. Luckily, you don't have to! One thing I often do is mix the ray-traced shadows with depth map shadows to create a more rounded appearance, with the depth map shadows providing the fuzzy edges and the ray-traced shadows making them accurate (Figure 4.36).

FIGURE 4.36 Here I mixed the depth map and ray-traced shadows in order to create a more natural appearance. Make sure you halve the intensity of the lights, however, if you do this.

Shaders and Materials

We have talked about shading, but now we need to understand what a **shader** is. Shading takes place when calculating the pixels in the spaces between the vertices (called polygon faces). The pixels get their RGB color value from the lighting information and the **material** information. A material is a series of channels that are applied to an object to create a final rendered appearance. A material uses a shader to know what channels of information are available to the user to change. Materials being used for GPU rendering are a lot different from materials being used for CPU software rendering, and generally must be treated very specifically for the intended output. This is mostly because the GPU, or real-time rendering system, can only handle a fraction of the calculations that are used in software rendering, and must be tailored to run as fast as they possibly can. We will be mostly covering materials and shaders as they are implemented in Autodesk's Maya software, which uses software rendering for its material editor, but keep in mind that shading and materials can be vastly different from one 3D program to another, and in fact, this is one of the areas that shows the greatest differentiation between them. This is mostly because they are using their own software-rendering engine, which requires certain channels of information to be calculated certain ways.

Shaders are mathematical formulae that take information from the light and the geometry normal, and convert it into color pixels on your screen. These shaders have been written to mimic the real-world properties of various appearances, the most important of which are shiny and non-shiny materials, also known as **specular** and **non-specular**. **Specularity** is the property of being shiny, or having **specular highlights**, which are places where the light reflects from the shiny surface and you see a bright white area and possibly a reflection. Figure 4.37 has two spheres that have been rendered in 3D. The sphere on the right has been rendered with a Lambert, or non-specular shader (sometimes known as a diffuse shader), while the sphere on the left has been rendered with a specular shader. Notice the circular area that is white on the sphere on the left. This is the specular highlight area, and it can make a surface look shiny just by virtue of having brighter pixels than the surrounding areas. The whiter and smaller the circular area, the shinier an object will appear to be. Examples of specular surfaces in real life are water, plastic, metal, and tile. Examples of non-specular materials in real life are plaster, stucco, paper, carpet, most clothing, and grass or dirt. Human skin is also specular (but it is much more

FIGURE 4.37 **(SEE COLOR INSERT)** The sphere on the left has a specular or "shiny" shader, while the sphere on the right has a non-specular shader.

complex than just that). It is important to note that reflection is a property of all specular surfaces in the real world; however, in 3D we can only achieve that with certain techniques, which will be discussed later.

Every software program has its own shaders, but there are "classic" shaders that are universal, and widely used in real-time engines. The shaders are generally split into two categories: specular and non-specular, and there are several listed next so that you can become familiar with their names, which are often derived from the person who first wrote the calculations for them.

Non-Specular Shaders

Lambert is the standard "diffuse-only" shader, which calculates the color values of the pixels without any calculation of reflection. It is the simplest shader, and used to render objects and surfaces that do not have any reflective or shiny properties at all. Figure 4.39 shows our two spheres with blue and red Lambert shaders applied.

Specular Shaders

Phong is the most commonly used specular shader. It is much like Lambert, except that it has a value and a color for the specular channels. Specular channels control the amount and color of the reflective brightness on an object. With cosine power, or specular size, Phong can control the size

FIGURE 4.38 **(SEE COLOR INSERT)** Images of various specular and non-specular objects.

FIGURE 4.39 **(SEE COLOR INSERT)** Lambert shaders do not have specularity.

of the circular specular highlight generated when light reflects from the source to the camera as well as the color of that reflected highlight. In Figure 4.40, you can see the basic diagram for a Phong shader, which is mathematically derived from the camera view of the scene and the light bouncing off of the object. While we do not really need to know all this "mathy" stuff, it is always nice to have a visual model of what is happening at the nuts and bolts level of anything we are working on. Figure 4.41 shows

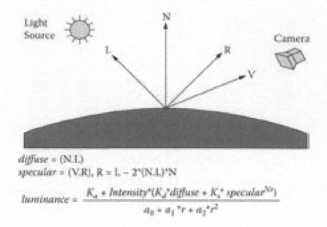

$$diffuse = (N.L)$$
$$specular = (V.R), R = L - 2^*(N.L)^*N$$

$$luminance = \frac{K_a + Intensity^*(K_d^*diffuse + K_s^* specular^{Ns})}{a_0 + a_1^*r + a_2^*r^2}$$

FIGURE 4.40 **(SEE COLOR INSERT)** Calculations for specularity on a Phong shader.

FIGURE 4.41 **(SEE COLOR INSERT)** The cosine power is higher on the right and lower on the left.

our two spheres again, this time with the shaders converted to Phong. The specular cosine power has been changed to a value of 2 on the sphere on the left (the blue one), and a value of 27 on the sphere on the right (the red one) to illustrate the resulting effect on the specular highlight. The smaller the cosine power, the bigger the area of the highlight. In addition to the cosine power, you can specify the RGB color of the specular highlight, which will be different for different types of surfaces. Metallic surfaces

FIGURE 4.42 **(SEE COLOR INSERT)** The sphere on the left looks more like gold, while the sphere on the right looks more like plastic. This is due to the difference in the specular color.

tend to reflect the same color light as the object, while plastics and glass or water will reflect a gray-scale color (mostly near-white). Figure 4.42 shows the two spheres, this time both rendered with a gold RGB color value, but one with the specular color as white, and the other with a specular color matching the RGB color. The sphere on the left looks more metallic because it has a specular color matching the diffuse color (appearing more like gold).

Blinn is an addition to Phong, in that more of the specular highlight can be controlled. It allows you to control the **eccentricity,** or spread of the circular highlight, as well as the roll-off, which is how fast from the center of the circle to the edge of the circle the brightness decreases. This added flexibility creates a more realistic depiction of shiny surfaces, and is the preferred shader for specularity in Maya. In Figure 4.43, you can see the same two spheres as before, but this time with a Blinn instead of a Phong shader, and the added control over the specular roll-off increases the level of realism when rendered.

Anisotropic is worthy of mention because it is commonly used to render objects that have multiple grooves, like a CD or a record. Because of the grooves in these objects, the effect shining back at the user can produce

FIGURE 4.43 **(SEE COLOR INSERT)** Blinn shaders have more sophisticated specular controls.

FIGURE 4.44 **(SEE COLOR INSERT)** The ball on the left is using Anisotropic shading.

very unique visual effects (like the rainbow reflection from a brand-new tea kettle) and must be specifically calculated in this special shader. Figure 4.44 shows the spheres again, this time with the sphere on the left having an Anisotropic shader. The specular highlight is greatly changed when there are multiple grooves in an object surface because the light conforms to the grooves differently.

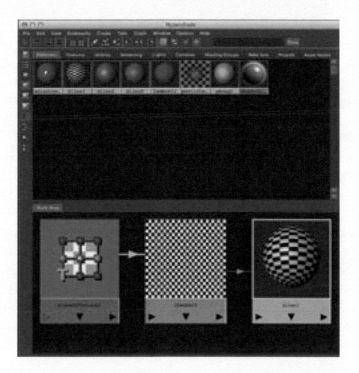

FIGURE 4.45 **(SEE COLOR INSERT)** The material editor in Maya (called the Hypershade). Often the materials are called shading *networks* because the information is stored in various *nodes,* which are then connected together to form a network.

Materials

Materials and **shaders** are oftentimes confused when talking about 3D graphics, and for good reason. They are often used interchangeably when talking about rendering graphics, but they are definitely not the same thing at all. A material is a network or stack of calculations that are managed in a render pipeline, which do all the calculations that convert the 3D and lighting information into pixels. Now that sounds a lot like a shader, but a material *uses* a shader to determine what channels are available to calculate and apply to an object in 3D. The material is what is assigned to the object, and this is assigned at the face level. Each polygon face has a number ID, which then is assigned a material ID, which is using a shader to calculate all those pixels. If it sounds confusing, then join the club. Rendering pipelines, materials, and shaders is probably the most technical and least "art-based" part of 3D graphics. The good news is that we do not have to know every little detail of the mechanics in order to set up good materials for our scenes. You do not need to know how spark plugs are manufactured in order to put a new set in your engine; you just need to know where they go and how to put them there.

Common Material Properties and Channels

Since we have multiple shaders that we can use in any given material, we will study the most common material channels and how they affect the outcome of the result. Materials work by calculating individual "channels" of data, which are in the form of RGB or alpha data. RGB uses three channels, each of which go from 0 to 255 in value. Mixing the values of these three channels together can create 16.77 million total different colors. Alpha values are only black and white values, which have a total of 256 different levels. Some channels only need alpha values, which take up less room and less time to calculate. Channels are calculated by the rendering pipeline in certain order, receiving some of the calculation equations from the shaders, which also determine which channels will be available to the user.

The standard material in most software-rendering-based 3D programs has the following key channels.

Color—Also known as the "diffuse" channel, this is as simple as it sounds. This determines the RGB color of the material, and this color is the basis of all further calculations. This is the only RGB value allowed in the material, with the exception of the specular color, and any other changes to the material channels will generally only change the lightness and darkness of that material on any object (unless it is specular and has specular color information).

Transparency—An object can be transparent or opaque, and this channel uses alpha data to determine if you can see objects behind it. In Maya, the white alpha value stands for transparent, while black stands for opaque, although many programs have this value reversed.

Ambient color—Ambient color is an RGB value that multiplies the RGB color value of the material with the lighting, which means that the higher the value, the brighter the object will appear, but it will include the light and dark areas of the light information. If the

FIGURE 4.46 **(SEE COLOR INSERT)** The ambient color value on the right sphere is turned up, which multiplies the value of the diffuse color after the lighting is calculated, which is why this sphere is red.

value is turned to completely white, the object with this material will appear uniformly in the RGB color value, but it will have areas of light and dark as defined by the lighting (however, the "dark" areas will be multiplied with the color value). In Figure 4.46, you can see a rendered image of our two spheres with the ambient color channel on the left-hand sphere set to 0, or black. In the sphere on the right side of the screen, you can see the ambient color value turned up to ~75%, or an RGB value of (175,175,175). Notice how the dark areas are red? The value of the ambient color is multiplied by the value to only the value of the diffuse color before rendering. Ambient color is a good channel to create effects where an object has a very bright surface but still needs to be affected by the lighting around it (like a low-emission light bulb). Sometimes ambient color value is known as self-illumination.

Incandescence—Incandescence is similar to ambient color, but the color value is multiplied on top of the lighting, which causes the object to get completely white when this value is turned up to white. The RGB color value is multiplied on top of the material color value and will wash out the lighting if turned up all the way. Figure 4.47 shows this effect, with the same values as the ambient color setting in Figure 4.46. Notice the difference in effect? The incandescent value multiplies all color information including lighting (instead of just the diffuse color

FIGURE 4.47 **(SEE COLOR INSERT)** Incandescence multiplies the value on top of the entire rendered sphere, making all of the pixels brighter at once.

channel), so it becomes white. Simulating self-illumination, however, does not actually light the objects in the scene; it just creates the illusion that the object for which you are setting up material properties is a source of illumination. You will still have to create a light or series of lights that send light out from that object's area. This can be done with the standard lights we have learned, or by using advanced lighting technique known as **area lighting**.

Bump mapping—Also known as **normal mapping**, the bump value uses alpha information from a **texture** (more on textures later) to create the illusion of "bumpiness" on a surface. It does so by creating fake normal information based on grayscale values to raise up or indent areas on your object. The advantage in using a bump map is that you can create very complex visual effects with a very small amount of geometry. Creating something like a ridged or textured appearance with bump maps instead of actual geometry is very efficient and the preferred way of handling this kind of effect. In Figure 4.48, you can see two panels side-by-side, on the left of which is a simple polygon plane, and on the right of which is that same plane with a material and a bump map applied. Despite only having a few polygons, this image shows how powerful the bump map can be in depicting real-life texture on an object. The grayscale values of the bump map create the high and low bumps and divots on the surface, which appear

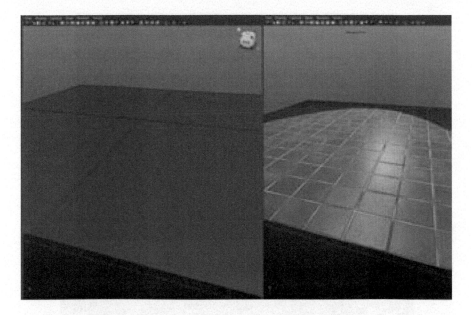

FIGURE 4.48 **(SEE COLOR INSERT)** Notice that the illusion of "texture" or dimples and grooves is created without heavy geometry. This is done using a bump map.

to be actually there, but in reality are created from faking extra normals generated from a texture containing alpha information. We will explore bump mapping in more detail in the exercise for this chapter, where we create the tile floor effect from a simple material and shading network.

Diffuse—Diffuse is the overall brightness of the color in the color channel. It is generally used to create areas where the surface of your object is "dirty" or where the color is duller than other areas. Dirt maps need to be very subtly created to identify areas of high and low color output, and these are usually painted onto a texture by hand in a 2D image editing program such as Photoshop (Figure 4.49).

Translucence—Translucence is the visual effect where an object is not transparent, but it allows light to pass through. This effect is evident if you hold something thin, like the leaf of a plant, up to a bright light. The light penetrates the leaf, but the leaf is not transparent. If you have an object with a translucent area, you can use this to recreate the visual effect. Figure 4.50 shows a scene with two spheres, the left of which has translucence on (reversed from our other figures thus

FIGURE 4.49 **(SEE COLOR INSERT)** Illustration of a dirt map in use.

FIGURE 4.50 **(SEE COLOR INSERT)** The sphere on the right has no translucency while the sphere on the left does.

far because the light source is in front of the spheres). Translucence depth is how far from the point of light the light will penetrate the object, and translucence focus is how far from the point of light penetration the light will spread (like falloff). Figure 4.51 shows the same scene as Figure 4.50, but with the translucency focus adjusted to have the light only partially shining through the object.

FIGURE 4.51 **(SEE COLOR INSERT)** The translucency focus has been increased to allow the light penetration to fall off over the surface.

Specular Material Channels

Remember, specular information is the bright circular highlights that stem from shiny objects. Anything that is changed here will alter the specular highlight portion of the rendered pixels. A Phong shader only has the cosine power, which controls the radius of the specular circle that will reflect from the light to the camera. The Blinn shader, however, allows you to edit the eccentricity and roll-off, which have greater control over the spread and "hotness" of the highlight.

Cosine power (Phong only)—As stated before, this channel controls the radius of the circular highlight.

Eccentricity (Blinn only)—Eccentricity is the Blinn equivalent of cosine power, and it also controls the radius of the specular highlight.

Specular roll-off—Specular roll-off controls the fading of the specular highlight from the epicenter to the edge. This controls how bright the specular color information is as it spreads out from the center.

Specular color—The specular color is an RGB channel that controls both the color of the specular highlight and the brightness of that highlight. One important tip about specular color—metallic objects (like gold) tend to emit the same color in their specular channels as the main color channel, while glossy objects (like a pool ball) tend to emit grayscale values (like grey to white). For this reason, the specular channel would be set to the color of the object if you want it to appear metallic or just plain white or near white if you want to depict a glossy object.

Reflection—Reflection is the amount, in a range of 0 to 1, a material reflects its surroundings, where 0 is not reflective at all and 1 is like a polished mirror. Reflections occur in two ways in Maya—with reflection maps, which are simulated reflections based on 3D textures (more on this later), or with ray tracing. Like calculating shadows, ray tracing does a calculation for every ray of light occurring in the scene for both casting shadows and reflecting objects in the surface of other objects. Ray tracing, when turned on, can be very expensive in terms of processing power, and for that reason is often the last solution to be used. Another thing to remember is that the reflection value is simply how "reflective" the surface is, and this value is only available when using ray tracing to calculate reflections or using a texture map in conjunction with a reflection map (for more information on this, see the Texture section of this chapter). You can use an alpha-value texture map to generate areas on a material that are more or less reflective. Figure 4.52 shows an example of two different reflectivity settings, with a value of 1 being a complete mirror and 0 being non-reflective. Figure 4.53 also shows the effect of using a texture map to determine reflective and non-reflective areas of the surface of an object.

Reflection color—Reflection color uses RGB information to tint the color of a reflection. It can also be used to create a reflection map, or an image that will appear to be reflected in the object with the material's surface. Reflection mapping is a technique used to simulate a reflection in order to save time and processing power by not using ray tracing, which is an expensive way to calculate reflectivity. Reflection mapping is also commonly used in real-time rendering, such as gaming, where the reflections are key in creating realistic lighting effects but they must be calculated at 60 frames per second (fps). Figure 4.54 shows an environment reflection map being used to enhance the realism of a reflective surface, without needing to calculate reflections through ray tracing.

FIGURE 4.52 **(SEE COLOR INSERT)** The sphere on the left has a reflection value of .3, while the sphere on the right has a reflectivity value of 1.

FIGURE 4.53 **(SEE COLOR INSERT)** An area has been defined telling the reflection where to be, and where not to be, using an alpha value to put a white square on a black background, white denoting a full reflective value and black denoting no reflectivity.

FIGURE 4.54 **(SEE COLOR INSERT)** The sky texture is placed as a reflection color on the sphere on the right, which "fakes" the reflection instead of using ray tracing to generate it.

WHAT ARE TEXTURES?

In computer graphics, we heard the term "texture" used a lot, but it is often poorly defined or explained, except to say that they are files the artist uses somehow to enhance the material information. Textures are, in fact, 2D images that are calculated in the many material slots we just talked about. Each of those material slots accepts alpha (black and white) or RGB data, which then gets calculated just like a color or value would. Texture maps can be external image files, which get loaded into the texture map channel, they can be **procedural**, or 2D images that are generated using mathematical formulas, which result in pixels. Procedural textures, unlike image files, can be changed, edited, and animated in real-time and can adjust their properties as part of your animation or scene. File textures are accessed externally, and must be linked to the particular texture channel slot by a "file" node or texture node, which contains information about how to process the information as it is calculated. Although there are usually some color correction tools and options for each file texture created, most of the information in a file image is derived from the file itself. Most pixel-image file formats are accessible, including the universal .jpg, .tif, .tga, and various other proprietary or less common formats. A movie sequence or movie file can also be used as a texture.

There are many different types of procedural texture generators in 3D programs, but the most common and heavily used are **noise generators** and **gradient generators**. One thing to keep in mind is that these are very general terms; that is, in each 3D program the terms will be slightly different. The important thing is to know what they do and what kind of images they can produce. Noise generation is the creation of randomness in a 2D image. There are usually several types of noise, which are generated by varying equations. Fractal is one of the most common types of noise, with Perlin and Marble being two other options. This random generation of pixels can be animated over time, which allows the information to be used for multiple applications. A ramp, or gradient, is another type of procedural texture, and it consists of a gradual change from one color to another. Ramps in Maya are very useful, and can be manipulated to generate all kinds of interesting effects. Figure 4.55 shows a ramp setup in Maya, which allows the user to gradually change from one color (or even another

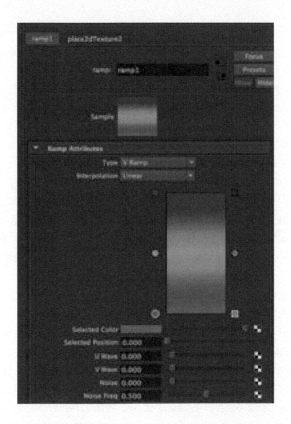

FIGURE 4.55 **(SEE COLOR INSERT)** A ramp texture in Maya.

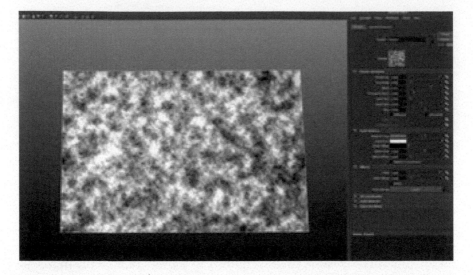

FIGURE 4.56 **(SEE COLOR INSERT)** A fractal texture with it applied to a polygon plane on the left.

texture) to another with varying levels of complexity. Figure 4.56 shows a fractal noise generated texture, which is one of several different randomizing textures that can be created procedurally.

Each 2D texture is placed into one of the material channels (as described earlier). Each material slot will be calculated into the shading "network" and rendered by the software or hardware rendering pipeline. Slots that take alpha information will be calculated as such, even if the image itself is RGB (only the grayscale values will be calculated).

Effective Texture Use

So now that we know what "textures" are and how they fit into the rendering pipeline and shading network, how do we use them? Most effective texture use is done by careful planning and tweaking essential elements of an object's material appearance to make it more realistic. Careful planning of the textures is necessary when generating or manipulating the texture image. The most important thing to consider, as a texture artist, is what kind of material properties your surface or object will have. What is it made out of? Is it metallic or plastic? Is it shiny or matte? Does it have a rough, indented, or raised texture? How does it react to the light? Is it reflective? Is it shinier in certain areas than others? Is the shine from the surface colored or white? Is it more reflective in certain areas than others? A good texture artist can deconstruct the appearance of an object and separate it into certain layers, which are then specifically tweaked and exported from an image program (like Photoshop) as individual texture maps, with the unique information encoded into each one.

The key to creating a great look for your surface is to use the three most important channels first: color, bump, and specularity (provided that your material is specular). In the exercise for this chapter, you will see how these three channels are vital for creating a rich, layered texture appearance to give the illusion of a complex surface without actually having anything other than a single polygon quad being rendered. The trick is to start with the color map—the most basic level of appearance—and work back from there. Figure 4.57 illustrates the completed rendering of an orange, which was textured using the three main channels—color, bump, and specular color. Figures 4.58, 4.59, and 4.60 are the color, bump, and specular color texture maps, respectively, which were used to generate the surface.

The color channel provides the basic color information about the object. In this case, what we really want to see is the organic shifting between the two prominent colors of the orange surface, which are orangish-red and orangish-yellow. It is possible to use a gradient to produce this appearance, but the regularity of the information would be less realistic than an actual photograph. One thing to note about using photographs of shiny objects for color information is that the natural specular highlights are mostly unwanted in a shading network because they are baked into the color channel and not dynamic, which means that they will not change with the

FIGURE 4.57 **(SEE COLOR INSERT)** The rendered orange with skin textures.

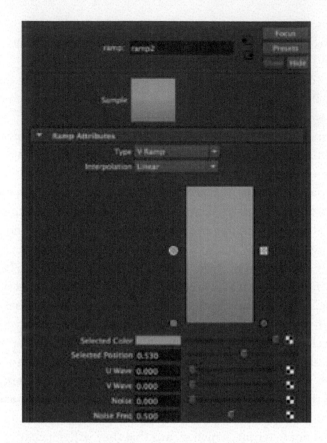

FIGURE 4.58 **(SEE COLOR INSERT)** A ramp was used to generate a soft gradient from darker orange to lighter orange.

light source. These highlights are most effective when put into the specular color channel, and are often removed from the color information by the texture artist.

The bump map, as we discussed earlier, creates the raised and indented areas of the object by simulating them by a process called **normal mapping**, which in simplest terms is creating vertex normal information to simulate more geometry than exists in the object you are rendering. Textured bump mapping uses alpha values to determine height. You can see that the black areas represent indented areas of a surface, while the white areas represent raised areas on a surface. Any gray areas will be the exact depth of the surface rendered. The orange bump map texture has tiny dark dots all over it because it is an indented surface, which you can see if you look closely at the skin of an orange.

FIGURE 4.59   This very stark contrast tiling texture map was made from a real orange skin photo. It is used as the bump map.

The specular color map is perhaps the most overlooked and underused type of texture map, but it is vital in creating realistic shiny objects. Most objects are not uniformly shiny at all. They are shinier in certain areas than in others. A specular color map will determine where the specularity is brighter or darker, but also its color as well. A tip for the RGB coloring of a specular highlight is that metallic objects generally have specular colors that are the same color as the metal, while glossy or shiny objects (such as our orange skin) have mostly white specular highlights. This is important when generating a specular map for metallic objects. Another thing to consider is that shiny objects tend to shine more in areas where they are raised up—the light hits the raised areas first, plus the raised areas are more likely to be brighter because they have more contact with objects that would polish them and keep them bright. This is not an absolute, but a general rule that allows us to use the bump texture map of a material as a starting place for our specularity map. Sometimes the fastest way to create a richer specular appearance is simply to copy the bump map into the specular map channel, which provides a minimal level of spec map that will shine brighter on the raised-up areas and darker on the divots. If you look at Figure 4.60, which is the specular map for the orange, you can see

FIGURE 4.60   A less contrast-heavy version of the bump map was used as the specular map. In this case, the shiny areas were not in need of stark differentiation because an orange is uniformly shiny. The higher areas, however, should be shinier than the divots because they are closer to the light.

that it is subtly different from the bump map (Figure 4.59), but it uses very similar data. Using the same bump and specular map can produce nice results, but varying the two slightly makes things even more realistic.

WHAT IS "UV MAPPING"?

UV Mapping

So now you know all about lighting, shading, materials, and textures. You thought we were done, right? That would be nice because it would be a lot easier to teach and understand, but unfortunately for us there is still one little problem—texture coordinates. Applying textures to materials is one thing, but getting them to show up on 3D objects is a completely different problem. The problem is that we have 2D texture maps that exist as flat images applied to 3D objects, which have coordinates in 3D Cartesian space. When you render anything to screen or image, you are rendering back to a 2D flat image, calculated in screen space. How do you know which pixels to put where? How is a flat image wrapped around a 3D object and re-rendered into pixels? This was the original question that

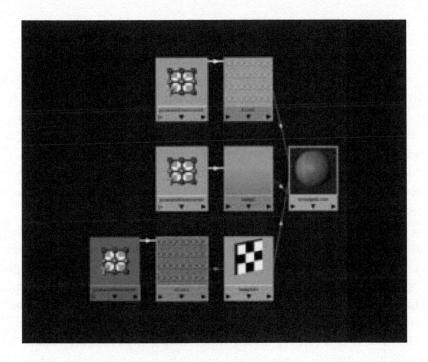

FIGURE 4.61 **(SEE COLOR INSERT)** A snapshot of the shading network as it appears in Maya. This is why they call it a network. It is many nodes for just one material.

early pioneers in 3D graphics faced, and the solution was the creation of a method of "mapping" pixels onto polygonal objects by placing the vertices and faces into a flattened space, known as "UV space," which is defined as the 2D plane upon which 3D objects are projected. The U-axis is the horizontal axis, and the V-axis is vertical (which is a nice mnemonic device to use if you get confused). NURBS have a natural U and V space because they are just flat planes to begin with, but polygons have no such mapping naturally. Without some way of determining where parts of images go on what objects, there really is no way of knowing what goes where. Good UV mapping is essential in creating proper materials for objects.

WHEN DO I NEED TO CREATE UV MAPPING?

UV mapping must be created when you have a polygonal object that has a material applied that uses any textures. Materials without any textures at all do not require UV mapping to be present, but there are very few instances where you will be creating a material that does not have any textures at all (although there will be somewhere this will be the case).

In addition, NURBS surfaces have inherent UV mapping coordinates based upon their nature, so you do not have to create UVs for them either. Polygon primitive objects are usually created with pre-existing UVs, so if you do not intend to alter them much from their intended state you will not need to generate new UVs. Any custom-modeled polygon object, however, or even a heavily altered primitive object, must have UV maps applied to it in order for any of the textures to be calculated when rendering. Objects like humanoid and organic creatures are some of the most difficult things to UV map due to the multiple planes and surfaces, and often a dedicated individual or team of individuals is necessary to create proper UV mapping for high-level games and cinema.

I know at this point in your learning experience you are probably getting frustrated. Don't panic. This is normal. UV space and mapping is, in my experience, one of the hardest things to get your head around in the 3D graphics world. It would be almost cruel of me to lay out all the technical aspects of UV mapping and coordinates without at least breaking here to say that this is not easy stuff to conceptualize. It took me 10 years to understand it, and I still struggle with putting it anywhere high on my list of priorities when it comes to creating art, which is usually reserved for the glamour jobs of modeling and animating. However, it needs to happen—you can't do much without good texture maps, and you can't have good texture maps without good mapping, and that takes a solid knowledge of UV space, UV mapping, and how to prepare for it from the very beginning. I cannot say that what you are learning here is going to make you a fabulous UV mapper—there are much better books out there for that kind of thing. However, I want to help you understand how it works, as well as the basic tools for creating and managing your UVs. At the very least, you should understand it.

A good visual tool for understanding UV mapping is the checkerboard texture, as it appears on different objects. In Figure 4.62, you can see a simple flat checkerboard texture, as it has been applied to a sphere, a cube (one repetition for each side), and a tube primitive. The less the texture stretches or warps, the better placed the coordinates are. Many artists use this checkerboard approach when laying out UV coordinates because it gives them a visual clue as to where they need to tweak the layout in order to keep distortion from happening. The sphere is the most difficult object to map properly because of the pinching possibility at the poles, which is solved with various methods in the mapping. Tiling of a texture map occurs in the parameters of the texture node, and it allows you to

FIGURE 4.62   Parade of the checkerboards.

FIGURE 4.63   Doubling the UV tiling makes the image duplicate itself in the horizontal (U) and vertical (V).

repeat the texture in the U and V as many times as you want, making patterns that are tileable (like floor tiles, brick walls, or floorboards) easy to adjust in scale to the environment. Figure 4.63 shows the effect of tiling the checkerboard texture several times on the same three objects as Figure 4.62.

HOW DO I CREATE UV MAPS?

Projections are the primary method of generating UV coordinates. A projection is the flattening of an object into U and V space. The idea of "generating" UV coordinates happens when each vertex is assigned at least one UV point. A vertex can have as many UV coordinates assigned to it as it has faces to which it is attached because each face can have its own separate "shell" or connected UV points. If this sounds confusing, it is! As you go through this segment, you will start to understand how it works. When creating a projection for an object (or a selection of faces), it is important to know your three main types of projections: planar, cylindrical, and spherical. These are the three main ways to project UV coordinates onto your models because they are the three most common uber-shapes of objects, which means that any surface or 3D model can be broken down into these three types of special relationships.

A plane is just that—a simple, flat plane onto which coordinates are projected. In Figure 4.64, you can see that I have a model of a soda can and texture for the top of the can. I have selected the faces of the top of the can and projected a planar UV mapping onto it, choosing the Y-axis. I have displayed the UV texture editor, where you can always see the relationship between the UV grid and the 3D object you are editing. This is important to understand where the individual pixels on your image file are

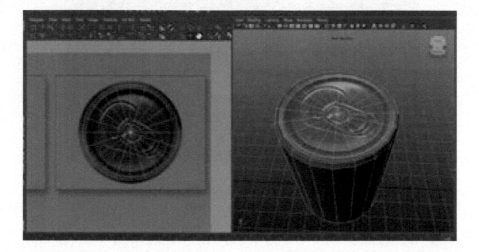

FIGURE 4.64 **(SEE COLOR INSERT)** The left side is the UV editor view, which displays the 2D texture image and the faces as they relate to it. The right-side view is the 3D view, where the pixels of the image are re-rendered on the 3D object as mapped out in the UV editor.

corresponding to the 3D sub-objects, and hence how they will be rendered on the screen. Figure 4.64 shows that relationship and how the planar project has slapped that image of a soda can top directly onto the selected faces. You can see that every pixel of the image is re-rendered to the screen in 3D, each pixel being told where to be rendered by its place in the UV coordinate space. The top of the can, which has been assigned a material with the associated texture in the color RGB channel, can now display the image when rendering the object.

A cylinder is a plane that has been wrapped around a tube, kind of like the label of a can. Cylindrical mapping takes the flat, square 2D image and "wraps" it around the selection of faces in a tubular manner. For this reason, I used it to create the mapping for the tubular part of the can, where the label would go. You can see in Figure 4.65 the selected faces, the texture map, and the resulting projection. Figure 4.65 has the UV texture editor and the faces as they are being projected. Notice that the top of the can is still showing up in the UV editor. The reason for this is that a single polygon object will reveal all UV coordinates, not just the one on which you are working. I have a material with the soda can texture assigned to the selected faces. The cylinder wraps the texture around the can by reversing the process. It unravels the selected faces based on the cylindrical shape and flattens them out along the UV texture coordinate space. This is very much like how a NURBS surface works, and if you understand that, you will have an easier time understanding how UV coordinates are generated.

FIGURE 4.65 **(SEE COLOR INSERT)** The 2D image of the can is wrapped around the cylindrical projection.

I applied the cylindrical UV projection to the selected faces, and as you can see in the following images the image of the can label easily wrapped around the full length of the can, based on a cylindrical shape. A cylinder is a very convenient tool for beginning your UV coordinates, especially for parts of models with cylindrical shapes like arms legs, and fingers.

Spherical UV projections are the final primary form of 3D projection shapes, and they are used almost exclusively for spherical or hemispherical objects. The main difference between this type of projection and the cylindrical is the "pinching" at the top of the object, generally known as the poles. The poles present a unique problem because in order to get them to appear properly, the texture map has to be carefully set up to stretch across the area without distorting. This is not a new problem—globe-makers have been dealing with it for years! This is why a flat map is not the exact image used to make the image on a globe. Instead, the map is deliberately warped to fit a spherical shape. Alternatively, in effect, as must be done in 3D, the flat map itself is altered in order to flatten out the proportions of a spherical shape, and the map is distorted to maintain similar proportions (because we know the Earth is round, right?). So here's the catch when looking at the pole of a spherical object/projection. Figure 4.66 is an image of a spherical-specific texture map of the Earth, as seen from space,

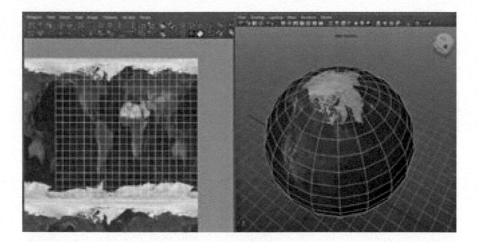

FIGURE 4.66 **(SEE COLOR INSERT)** The "saw-tooth" UV coordinates allow each triangle to have its own set of UV points, making the spread even on this texture.

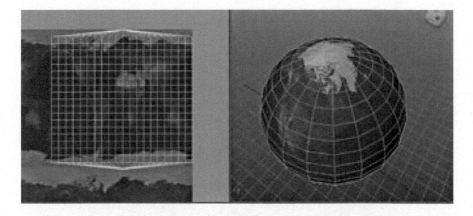

FIGURE 4.67 **(SEE COLOR INSERT)** The pinched UV coordinates at the poles of a sphere create only a single UV point for all the triangles at the poles, which result in warped texture coordinates.

with images of the UV projection and the coordinates in the UV editor. The little pieces at the end are called "saw-tooth" because they resemble a saw. What is occurring at the poles is that the vertex, which connects all of the triangles, has multiple UV points created for it (one for each triangle to which it is connected). Those points all line up to keep the pixels from being stretched too thin (called streaking) across the triangles if there were only a single UV point, as you can see in Figure 4.67, which illustrates what this would look like without the saw-tooth.

It is a good time to point out here that pixel streaking is a huge problem for 3D beginners when they apply texture maps or make botched attempts at generating UV mapping for an object. The tendency is to just click the "project" button when trying to get a texture to show up on an object without planning it out. Another common pitfall is to have bad triangulation or modeling issues, which cause extremely long triangles to be formed on a model. This causes the pixels to streak or warp when the rendering engine is trying to figure out what to put where. Properly setting up UV coordinates is a lengthy and difficult process, and most definitely needs to be approached with a plan. A good word of advice is to put some thought into the different flat planes your surface consists of, and where the best places to sew those planes together will be. Figure 4.70 shows an example of how poorly plotted UV points can result in distorted and streaked pixels in the 3D rendering.

FIGURE 4.68 **(SEE COLOR INSERT)** An unobscured view of the saw-tooth UVs from Figure 4.66.

FIGURE 4.69 **(SEE COLOR INSERT)** An unobscured view of the pinched pole UVs from Figure 4.67.

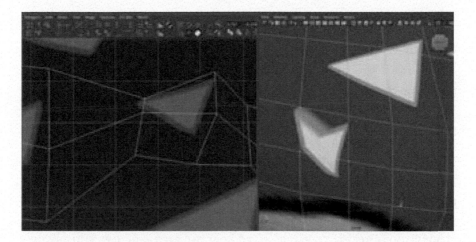

FIGURE 4.70 **(SEE COLOR INSERT)** The poor UV layout on the left results in distortion and streaking on the right.

HOW DO I CREATE MORE COMPLEX UV MAPPINGS?

UV mapping can be edited point by point in any UV editing window, which most 3D content creation software will provide. One thing to mention here is that game developer middleware, most significantly Unity 3D and Unreal Engine, do not have built-in UV editors (although plugins might exist). Usually UVs and polygons are sent to game developers already complete.

Although advanced UV editing is a science unto itself, and it falls outside the scope of this book, it is important enough to mention it in order to understand the *mechanism*, if not fully learn the techniques. It takes some time and practice to understand fully the relationship between UV space and how a texture appears on your 3D object, and even longer to be able to perform the more advanced UV editing that is necessary to properly texture complex organic objects. What the beginning 3D student *should* understand, however, is how to avoid poor UVs which will result in stretching, streaking, and distortion of the texture as it is rendered in 3D. If you follow the exercise in Chapter 3, which takes you through the process of creating UV coordinates for an object, you will get a clear understanding of how to create proper UVs on an object.

HOW DO I RENDER AN IMAGE?

Software Rendering

Here we are—the final output. You have your lights, you have your materials, you have your texture maps, and they are properly UV mapped. How then, do you go about turning all of that into an image file? This is where software rendering comes into play.

Thus far, we have just been seeing our objects and things in our preview window through hardware rendering, which is a good way to judge basic elements of our scene. However, the real test of high-level image production for video or film is to software render it into an image. One thing to note, however, is that this is completely different than creating these elements for a real-time game. Remember, we are using two entirely different methods of production. Software rendering happens when you open your render view (called different things in different 3D programs) and hit the render button. The program, called a "rendering engine," of which there are several options, will compile all of your objects, materials, textures, and any post-processing elements like fog or optical effects, and then calculate pixels based on all of this information, through the camera or cameras you have set up, and ultimately spit out a single or series of still images. Sounds complex, doesn't it? It is. There are some people whose job it is to do nothing else but set up, tend, and manage renders as they happen. It is a big part of the video and film production process, but it is not always a glamorous job. It is another one of those little things about the 3D graphics industry that is overlooked often but takes up an incredible amount of time.

There are several mechanics of rendering to an image that you should at least understand, even if you do not intend to muck around with the minutia of render settings. Everyone needs to know certain aspects of the rendering process in order to check their own work, so I will list several vital aspects of rendering that you should know.

Rendering engine—The rendering engine is the specific piece of software that turns all of your geometry, lights, and material networks into a still image, or sequence of still images. Most major software packages offer a variety of rendering engines to use. Maya, 3D Studio Max, and Softimage all have proprietary software rendering images, with the option also to use Mental Ray. Mental Ray is an independent rendering engine that reproduces complex physical-based lighting simulations on top of higher-level volumetric effects. Since most rendering is very software-specific, I will not go into render settings and such in detail, but it begs at least a brief discussion and illumination on the process and quality levels available. Each rendering engine will be able to do specific things that will enhance the final rendered image, making it far higher quality than your interactive real-time rendering engine can possibly achieve. The more detail and quality you seek, however, the longer the rendering will take. Some high-def high-quality images can takes hours each. Therefore, setting up rendering requires serious attention paid to efficiency on top of quality. Some of the common options most major rendering engine possess are listed here, in order to make you aware of the options and their effect on the final output and length of time it will take.

Resolution—This is the pixel resolution of an object, and the higher you go, the more calculation time it will take to generate it. One tip is to keep your test renders to smaller resolutions in order to cut down your rendering times.

Multi-pass filtering—Sometimes known as "anti-aliasing," this parameter softens the jagged lines of textures and rendered images in order to enhance the final output. This drastically slows down your render times, and it is more of a global than a local option (which means it requires a lot less tampering or adjusting), so the best option is to keep it off until the final render.

Motion blur—Motion blur is the phenomenon of fast-moving objects appearing to be rendered in several areas at once with varying levels of transparency. This blur is the result of the object moving faster than the shutter speed and leaving a "ghost" trail as it is partially picked up by the exposure. In 3D, it must be simulated in either 2D or 3D. 2D motion blur is fast and simple, being good for simple effects on single objects that do not have transparency. More complex scenes, and especially ones that are going out to cinema films like *Star Wars*, demand high-level accuracy in motion blur calculation and must use 3D motion blur, which simulates the shutter speed of the camera (which is adjustable). 3D motion blur, however, will often double to triple your rendering times so use it only if you must.

Ray tracing—Shadows and reflections can be calculated separately, and you can determine how many iterations or levels of calculations you want to provide for each. The higher the level, the more accurate and smoother the resulting images, but of course, it will exponentially increase your rendering times. Generally, a good strategy is to test render at the lowest levels and move up if necessary to improve image quality.

EXERCISE: CREATING A COMPLEX MATERIAL

Step 1: Set up Scene and Lighting

Start a new scene in Maya. The first thing we will do is create a simple polygon plane and a light in the scene (so that we can see the specular highlight a little better). Create a primitive polygon plane and size it to match the entire grid (Figure 4.71). You will also create a directional light and rotate its X-axis to a value of –135. This is all the geometry we need for the scene. We will do the rest in materials. The texture maps used in this exercise are available on the website.

Step 2: Creating a Material Network and Assigning It to Your Object

Now that we have set up the scene to preview our materials, we will need to create a new Blinn material. Open the Hypershade and choose Create > Materials > Blinn. A new material with a Blinn shader will be created in the Hypershade. "tile_MAT" is what you should name this new material.

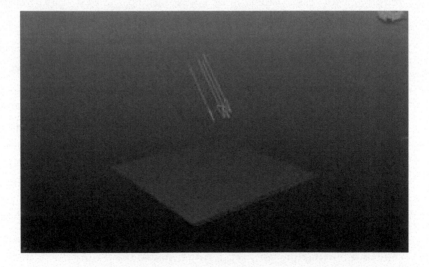

FIGURE 4.71 **(SEE COLOR INSERT)** Poly plane and directional light at an angle.

The "_MAT" is useful in denoting objects of type material, and is a very good practice when you eventually work with highly complex scenes. Now we need to apply our material to the polygon plane in our scene. Select the object in the scene, and right-click over the material in the Hypershade and choose "apply material to selection" from the marking menu that pops up in the window. This will apply the material to the object so that you may see it in the 3D perspective view. You will also make sure to set your perspective view renderer to "high quality" if you are using a Mac, or "Viewport 2.0" if you are using a PC. This will allow you to see bump and specular textures interactively in the perspective window. Also, make sure that you choose "hardware texturing" and "use lighting" for the shading options (keyboard shortcuts "6" and "7," respectively). This will also ensure you can see hardware textures and lights in your scene.

Step 3: Editing your Material

When we edit materials, we generally do it with the Hypershade and the attribute editor (Figure 4.72). Make sure that they are both open so that you are able to quickly make changes in the material settings.

In order to make this material, you will need to download the textures available on the website. The first file you will need to download is the

FIGURE 4.72 **(SEE COLOR INSERT)** Hypershade and attribute editor open in Maya.

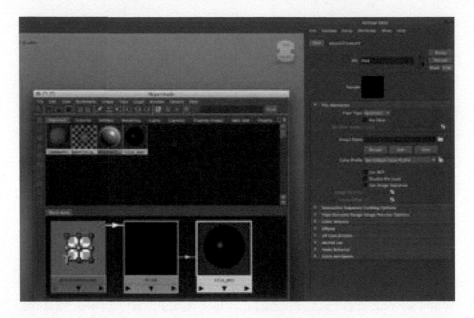

FIGURE 4.73 **(SEE COLOR INSERT)** Creating the file texture.

tile_color.jpg image. We will be loading that into the color channel of the material, by clicking on the tiny checkerboard on the right of the color channel in the attribute editor. A new window will pop up, asking you to define what kind of texture you will be using. Choose "File" and two new nodes will be created, a "fileTextureNode" and a "place2DTextureNode." You can access the material network by right-clicking over the material node in the Hypershade and choosing "graph network," which will graph the shader network in the panel below, as you can see in Figure 4.73.

Choose the tile_color_map.jpg, as shown in Figure 4.74, for the file here. This will load it into the material and display it on the shader ball in the Hypershade as well as on the polygon plane in your scene. Select the "place2DTextureNode" and change the U and V tiling levels to 3. This will multiply the times the texture is repeated on any object assigned this material (Figure 4.75). The place2DTextureNode is always created with every texture, and it contains all information pertinent to the placement of the texture in 3D space as far as it affects the image. However, it does not change the actual UV coordinates of the object itself.

Next, you will create a new file texture, this time in the bump map channel. Choose tile_texture_bump.jpg in the file location dialogue (Figure 4.76). You will notice that when you create a bump map texture, it

FIGURE 4.74 **(SEE COLOR INSERT)** Color tile texture map.

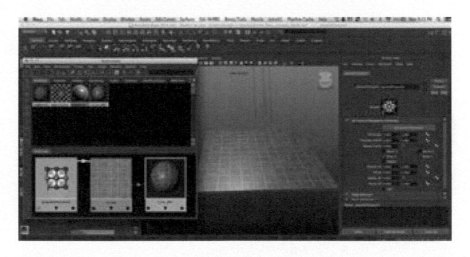

FIGURE 4.75 **(SEE COLOR INSERT)** Repeating color tile texture on object.

not only creates a file node and a place2DTextureNode, but it also creates a bump2D node. This extra node has all the information about the "fake" normal of the object, which will be generated by the black and white information from the texture map you chose. Select the bump2D node and change the bump depth to around .3, which will give you a reasonable

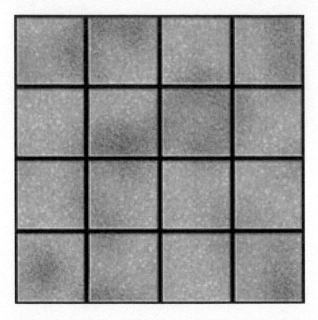

FIGURE 4.76   The bump map is always an alpha, or grayscale value texture.

height/depth ratio of the black and white values you are seeing on the texture map. Next, make sure that the place2DTextureNode for the bump map texture has been tiled 3 in the U and V settings as well, so it will match the color map. It should create a "crunchiness" to the image, where the brighter parts will be raised up on the surface and the darker parts will have divots, as you can see in Figure 4.77.

The last important map to create is a specular color map. This tells the object where to be shiny, and what color to shine. The specular color map channel accepts RGB information, but unless your object is metallic or a special case, the specular color emitted will be mostly white. Therefore, we will plan to make the bump map texture play double-duty here, and middle-mouse drag it onto the specular color channel from the Hypershade. This is a sure-fire trick to spice up your specular bump materials because the bumpiness of an object gives it a natural place where the light will reflect and where it won't—the raised areas will be shinier and the lower areas will be less shiny. Since this is a tile floor, the grouting will not shine at all. All of this makes it a great place to simply copy over the bump map into the specular color map (Figures 4.78 and 4.79).

And now you can congratulate yourself! You have put together a complex material appearance with a couple of simple texture maps. What was

FIGURE 4.77 **(SEE COLOR INSERT)** Look how much detail we can get with a bump texture map. It looks like a much more complex piece of geometry.

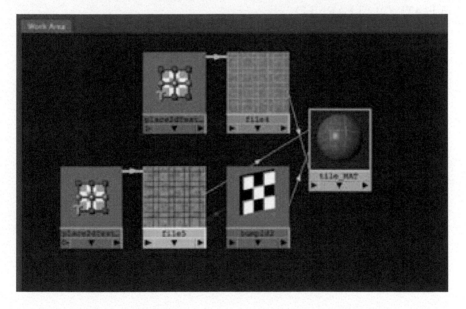

FIGURE 4.78 **(SEE COLOR INSERT)** The completed shading material network.

once a single polygon plane has now taken on the appearance of a gritty, shiny, and complex tile floor. The important lesson to take away from this is that much of the visual complexity of your work can be completed in materials, and does not have to be done in the geometry. The rule of thumb is always go for the simplest method of creating the best result.

FIGURE 4.79 **(SEE COLOR INSERT)** The completed real-time render. The specular map is subtle but makes a big difference.

WHAT YOU LEARNED

- Creating textures

- Editing UV tiling

- Creating bump maps

- Using textures in more than one material channel

CHAPTER 5

Animation

WHAT IS ANIMATION?

Definition and Basic Concepts

Animation, in its simplest definition, is change over time. Anything that we see on TV, games, or film that is not captured from video is considered animation. The distinction between video and animation is that video and film are "captured" images from real life, while animation images are "generated" either by hand or by a computer. Animation images are played back at a certain rate and movement is created (Figures 5.1 and 5.2).

The speed at which the animation is played back will greatly alter the speed at which the eye interprets that animation. Twenty-four fps is the standard **real-time** speed of animation. This is the speed at which film is played when you go to a theater. It is considered real-time because this is very close to the speed that our eyes process images. Therefore, if you film a person walking across a room at 24 fps, and then play it back at the same speed while the person walks across the room at the same speed, they will both arrive at the same place at the same time. If you were to capture the same movement at a different speed or play it back at a different speed, the actual person would not be in sync with the film person. The pioneers of cinematography (Figure 5.3) and the creation of film spent a lot of time working with high-speed capture of human and animal motion so that they could play it back and determine these kinds of factors.

Other animation speed formats, and ones that are important to note, are 30 fps, which was most widely used in pre-LCD and pre-HD screens

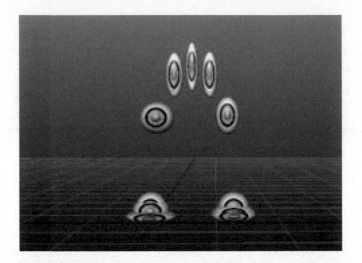

FIGURE 5.1 **(SEE COLOR INSERT)** Bouncing ball animation with ghosting.

FIGURE 5.2 **(SEE COLOR INSERT)** Ghosted character animation.

for NTSC video interlaced format, and 60 fps, which is widely used in gaming for 60-Hz LCD and HD screens. If the screen refreshes itself 60 times per second, then the best frame rate to be generating or replaying images is 60 fps, instead of 24 fps because the motion will be smoother. If this sounds confusing, don't despair. It is confusing for everyone in the

FIGURE 5.3 Muybridge was an early pioneer in photography and study in animal and human motion.

industry and frame rate of animation vs. frame rate of output is always a cause for concern. The best way to deal with this is to make the determination beforehand and choose a method from there. It is very important to understand frame rate and how it will affect the ultimate outcome of your work when you are done.

On great thing about working with computers is the scalability of your work. When choosing the frame rate of animation, you can be confident that it will not be very difficult to change to a different frame rate while keeping the same relative timing of your animation. Most 3D animation programs have the ability to shift the time scale while retaining relative time between the keyframes. While this does not get you off the hook for not pre-planning your animation project, it should at least give you some flexibility to fix a project if you realize at some point your 24 fps animation needs to be changed to 30 fps. Manually adjusting all the keyframes to fit the exact same timing would be very time-consuming, but when dealing with a computer it is generally simple. The most important thing to remember is that ultimately you will be playing this animation via some device, be it digital video, DVD, film, or in a game.

For all purposes in this book, we will plan to use the time scale of 30 fps, for the reason that it is a more scalable frame rate than 24 fps. If you are developing for digital output (YouTube or streaming) or if you are developing for a game, this is more convenient than 24 fps, which is only used in film.

HOW DO YOU ANIMATE?

Keyframes and Keyframing

Animation happens when you save an attribute's values at a certain time, and then save a different value at a different time. The values change over the time elapsed between them, between the first value and the second value. This saved value at a particular point in time is called a **keyframe**. The change in value over the period of time in between the keyframes is called **interpolation**. These keyframes and values are expressed in a simple graph, as you can see in Figure 5.4.

The X, or horizontal axis, represents time, while the Y, or vertical, axis represents value. The two points represent two keyframes, and the curve in between them is called a **motion curve**. The motion curve is derived from two very important elements: interpolation, which is the creation of values based on the keyframes, and keyframe **tangents**, which are the Bézier handles used to determine the shape of the curve. The places where the curves intersect the graph are the values that are generated by interpolation. Interpolation creates values in between keyframes, where there are no saved values, but there are implied values because we know that the values will change as time moves (moving forward at 30 fps). Therefore, for every keyframe that occurs, your computer is interpolating the value of your attribute based on where that motion curve is. So you can see in Figure 5.5 that the

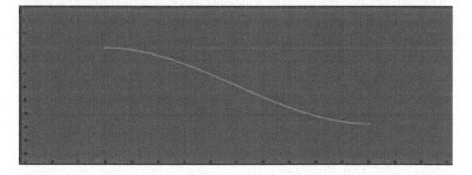

FIGURE 5.4 The points on this graph are keyframes, or saved value at a point in time. This forms a simple graph, with time being horizontal and value being vertical.

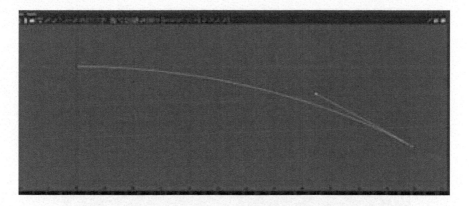

FIGURE 5.5 The values between the keyframes are determined by interpolation, which is determined by the shape of the curve.

motion from Figure 5.4 was a translate X motion, which was interpolated to move from one point in space to another over 30 frames, which equals 1 second.

WHAT CAN I ANIMATE?

You can animate pretty much anything that has a numerical value in most software packages. Anything that has a value in a 3D package can be animated. The most commonly animated properties in what we generally consider "animation" are transforms of objects. However, animation is not limited to just transforms. One thing that is important in becoming a good animator is to think about everything as being able to be animated. This makes it possible to include subtle actions that raise the bar of the animation. Character animation is done mostly through the rotation of transforms, most specifically the rotation of joints that make up the skeleton of the character. Figure 5.6 shows a character and a skeleton, which is mostly controlled by animation of the rotation of the skeletal joints.

WHAT ARE THE DIFFERENT METHODS OF ANIMATING?

Animation has many purposes. You can animate characters for games and for film. You can animate a fly-through for previewing architectural designs. You can animate robotic equipment for mechanical renderings. You can even animate subatomic particles for the 3D visualization of data from the Hadron Super-Collider (that was a discussion I once had with the Physics Department at a college that had a NASA grant). *What* you animate and for what purpose will determine *how* you animate. Animation

FIGURE 5.6 **(SEE COLOR INSERT)** A character rigged with joints that are animated by rotation. (Character design and model by Bert Farache, rig and skeleton by author.)

needs to be approached, like everything else in 3D graphics, with a lot of pre-planning and forethought. Next are some methods of creating and organizing animation data.

Pose-Based Animation

The classic method of character animation, and my personal choice when doing most organic motion, is to use the time-honored tradition pioneered by great animators like Walt Disney and others in the 1920s and 1930s. Pose-based animation is a great way to start learning how to animate characters and character-like objects (which we are going to do in the exercise at the end of this chapter). It is also a great way to understand how animation applications were first brought to the computer. You see, in the old Disney days of animation, there had to be a master animator and an apprentice animator. The master animator would draw the main poses of the character animating, such as you see in Figure 5.7. The master animator would take these drawing to the apprentice animator, who would then slave away late into the night (much like your author is doing right now) drawing the "tween frames" or all the steps in between the main poses. Remember, in film it takes 24 images per second to make a real-time moving object, so every second of animation requires 24 drawings. Sometimes animators (Hanna-Barbera is a great example of this) chop the

FIGURE 5.7 **(SEE COLOR INSERT)** Early cell drawings of cartoon characters would be done in "key poses" or important breaks in movement. The apprentice would frantically sketch in all the "tween poses." (Courtesy of artist, Topher Putnam.)

amount of images into 12 fps and "double-up" on frames, which means they display each frame twice and play it at 24 fps. This is mainly done to save time doing those tedious drawings. However, the lower the frame rate, the lower the overall quality of the cartoon.

Now when early animation software was being developed, you can see how the animators, who were coming from traditional methods, might look at the computer as an animation tool. The saw it as a way to save time and work. Essentially the computer becomes your apprentice animator, slaving away and doing all the work late into the night while you relax by the pool. Or so we would hope. However, the truth is technology in terms of saving us time and energy just added all kinds of new layers on top of what we already had to contend with. It became the animator's job to set up the master key poses, now called "keyframes," and the computer's job to do all the work in between. Only now, we have to come in and make the computer's work look less mechanical and boring (more on how to do this later).

So now, we come to the setting of the "key poses." Key poses are strong, definitive moments in kinetic action. Every time a character performs an "action" or makes a movement, certain points in that action are visual clues into what is happening. In animation, like in all art, there is a certain need for exaggeration or an over-statement of what is happening. Because animation is a recreation of reality, it needs a little bit of over-the-top appearance to make it read well on the screen to the human eye. This is like how actors exaggerate their emotions on screen—they need to over-emphasize the occurrence for the viewer to feel the impact. We could all use a little drama in our life!

There are two types of basic classic animation setups: single action and cycles. Single actions are things that are done once, and looping animation is repetitive action that you can have happen exactly the same way, repeatedly. A single action is a baseball pitch being thrown, and a cycle is a person walking, running, or swimming. Single actions can be strung together to create a complete character animation, and they can also be mixed with cycle animations, as long as the points in between match up to make a transition.

Both single action and cycle animation are done with five main poses: rest, anticipation, action, follow through, and rest (again). The poses run in that order for single actions, but are shifted a bit in cycling animations (more on that later).

Let's look at this like we are at a baseball game and watching the pitcher on the mound. The pitcher stands at rest, preparing to throw the ball. **Rest** is our first pose, where he is a body at rest, just hanging out there, doing nothing (Figure 5.8).

FIGURE 5.8   Pitcher at rest, preparing to throw the pitch. (Image by Atoine Letarte, CC BY 3.0.)

FIGURE 5.9 Pitcher winding up to throw, coiling like a spring to generate kinetic energy.

Then he winds up, which is **anticipation,** or the preparation for a kinetic action (Figure 5.9). He is preparing to throw that ball at 100 miles per hour, so he needs to wind his body up tightly in order to deliver that amount of energy. Now I realize most of the time humans do not make such exaggerated kinetic anticipation to do something (imagine winding up to staple your homework). However, there is a significant need to prepare for any strong kinetic action, like throwing a punch or swinging a sword around. You must create some kind of initial movement in order to perform an action, usually in the reverse of that action. In animation, we need to really exaggerate that wind-up because it creates an action, like a rubber band, which telegraphs to the viewer what to prepare for next. Without that wind-up, the animation will end up looking flat and lifeless. Watch some Pixar movies, and you will see some great anticipatory action, which is why they have such life-like characters.

Action is the next step in the process. The action is what this whole thing is about—it defines the animation. This is the maximum point of kinetic release. If you were jumping, it would be the top of your jump. If you were our pitcher, it would be the moment the ball is released from the hand, like in Figure 5.10.

Follow-through is what happens when you release all of that kinetic energy. If you can throw a baseball 100 mph (and I can't), your body isn't going to just stop on a dime. It will continue to move, even if you try

FIGURE 5.10   A 100 mph fastball. That is a lot of kinetic energy. The pitcher is using his arm like a giant pendulum, just about to release the ball at the end of that pendulum swing.

to stop it. Making a strong kinetic action requires that your body continues through that arc until gravity, friction, or the dampening effect of muscles and bones absorbs the energy. That is why the pitcher is always in that crazy position right after the pitch—he has released so much kinetic energy throwing the ball that fast that his body can't just stop right after he releases the ball; it has to keep going until the energy is dispersed by the body's natural shock-absorber (Figure 5.11).

Now we are back to **rest**. Once the kinetic energy has dispersed, the body is once again at rest. If you are animating another action happening right after this one, then you might have rest as more of a transition—the point between one kinetic action and another. In classic animation, you can string together one action and another in a sequence, with the second rest post being the point in between. Game animations often have this pose the same for almost all animations, so that each can be triggered by the user as they occur and you can have a seamless transition between one and another. Sports games, like football, basketball, and baseball all have thousands of animations, which rely on having one or more rest poses the player can transition between when the game is going.

Cycling an animation is all about creating a loop that can be played continuously. If you have ever seen any of those old Hanna-Barbera cartoons like the Flintstones or Scooby Doo, or even Warner Brother's Bugs

FIGURE 5.11   It looks funny but this is how Major League Baseball pitchers end up after the throw. You cannot just stop right after you deliver that heavy amount of kinetic energy. You have to keep going until the energy is absorbed through you and into the ground.

Bunny, you have seen plenty of animation cycles. Any animation of a character walking, running, or repeating an action (like pumping one of those railroad carts) is a cycle. It is very similar to a single-action animation, with the difference that the start and end position is always the same, allowing the animator to play it on a loop and make the character appear to be moving with some form of locomotion. The nice thing about cycling animations is that they only have to be animated once, and can then be played endlessly anywhere you need the character to be moving in the story. Typically, the action pose is the initial pose, and then the rest of the poses cycle afterward, alternating left and right if the character is humanoid or a quadruped. Figure 5.12 shows a typical cycle animation action. (See also Figures 5.13 and 5.14.)

FIGURE 5.12   The same sequence as the pitcher, only simplified—rest, anticipation, action, follow-through, and rest again.

FIGURE 5.13 3D man running. Notice how the beginning and end frames are in a similar position, which is what makes this animation cycleable.

FIGURE 5.14 The steps in a very simple "bounce" animation, where the first and last poses are identical. This is a shift from Figure 5.12, in which the rest poses were removed. If played on a loop, this animation will continuously cycle.

WHAT ARE OTHER WAYS TO ANIMATE?

Rotoscoping and Motion Capture

Rotoscoping is an animation method that takes live video or film and animates the character or action on top of the live action. Ralph Bakshi made good use of the technique in his popular films during the late 1970s and early 1980s, and there is a great Betty Boop cartoon widely available online with Cab Calloway as the rotoscoped reference for the ghost walrus rendition of Minnie the Moocher. One of the nice things about rotoscoping is that it provides you with detailed, real-time motion, which you can use to match timing and keyframing. This is completely different from pose-based animation because your main goal is to match the underlying live video, which has subtleties of movement that are very hard to match when doing pose-based animation. Rotoscoped animation has a decidedly

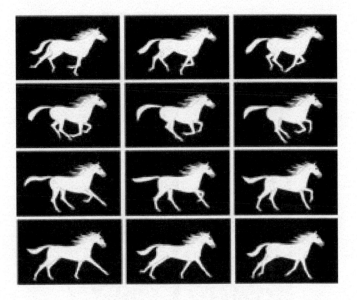

FIGURE 5.15   Horse animation, which was hand-drawn over video footage.

different feel from pose-based animation, and an experienced animator can spot it right away. Generally, the action is matched with heavy keyframing or what I like to call the "brute-force" technique, where you create many keyframes to match each frame of the film action you are matching. Not only do you have to set tons of keyframes, but also it is very time-consuming . In Figures 5.15 and 5.16, you can see the technique of rotoscoping put to good use for a very difficult motion to animate, which is that of a galloping horse.

Motion capture is the last animation technique we will discuss. Motion capture involves the 3D capture of human motion onto a skeleton using one of several techniques, generally with a body actor wearing magnetic or optical data points on a suit. This motion is tracked and converted to skeletal joint rotation data, and then run through a "solver," which determines where these joints are based on algorithmic data, and converted into keyframes. It is the most data-dense form of animation, consisting of thousands and thousands of keyframes, usually one for every frame. Motion capture for film characters was best exemplified when Andy Serkis played Gollum, which is probably one of the best-known digital characters ever to grace the silver screen. Motion capture is one of the least time-consuming ways to animate because there is no initial animation time at all. It all is captured in real-time. No animator is needed. The time it saves in animation, however, generally is eaten up in setup time and fiddling with

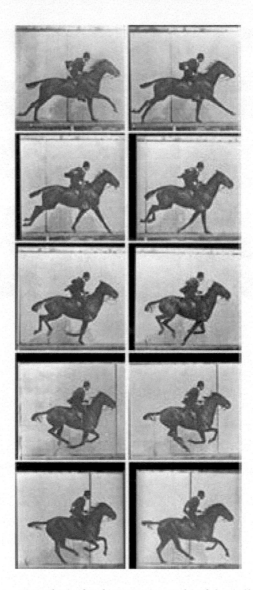

FIGURE 5.16 The original Muybridge motion study of the galloping horse.

multiple solutions to get the motion to solve accurately. It also requires an animator to take the initial data and turn it into a useful animation, so you don't save a whole lot of time in the end, but you do have a vastly different methodology of production. Motion capture studios that have solid setups tend to get the most out of this type of animation process, and I feel small studios are better off exploring hand-keyframed animation (Figures 5.17 and 5.18).

FIGURE 5.17   Motion capture actor in the motion capture studio with suit on.

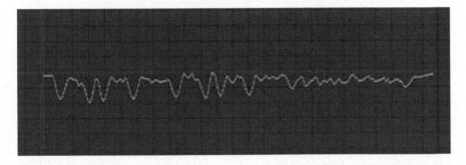

FIGURE 5.18   Motion capture data in a graph editor. The data is very dense due to a keyframe being generated per frame.

HOW DO I CREATE GREAT HAND-KEYFRAMED ANIMATIONS?

Editing Your Motion Curves

Now we know how to *create* keyframes based on pose animation, and we know what those keyframes should be, but we still do not have the total package. You see, the problem with motion, especially organic kinetic motion, is that it does not happen at a constant rate. In Figure 5.19, you can see a robot arm that has been rigged with a simple skeleton that

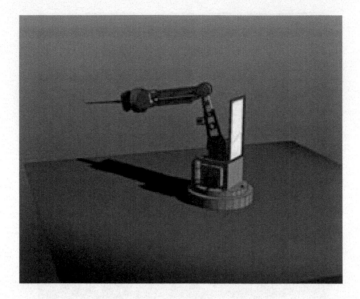

FIGURE 5.19   Robot arm rigged.

you can rotate. This robot arm does not need to create kinetic energy. It gets its movements from a series of motors and hydraulic pumps, which are all controlled by a computer. If this robot arm moves around, you will clearly see that it is a robot. The motion will look stiff and "robotic" (you see, we even have a term for this type of motion!). Now, you have to ask yourself, why does the motion look this way? What differentiates the robotic movement from more natural organic motion? Well, for one thing, human movement uses that rubber-band action we talked about previously. It winds up, generating energy, then releases it and continues to follow through that energy until the momentum is absorbed. A robot does not do any of that—it moves slowly and steadily *at the same rate.* The rate at which the action happens is very important because I can move from one point to another over a period of 1 second, but as a human, I will have moments of **acceleration** and **deceleration**, as opposed to a robot, which would have the same speed the entire action.

Think about it like this—you and I are racing cars, we both leave at the same time, and we both cross the finish line at the same time. During the 60 seconds it takes us to get there, I took off like a bat out of hell at a rate of 100 mph and you only took off at 60 mph. However, during the course of the race, I had to slam on my brakes a few times to avoid losing control and you steadily increased your speed. We both arrived at the same place at the same time, but the distance we had traveled from the beginning would have been vastly different at any given time during the race *except* at the finish line, when we both crossed at the same time. This is because our acceleration and deceleration varied greatly, even though our end and beginning positions were the same. Remember our motion graph we discussed earlier? Well, the motion of the cars in the race would look a lot like Figures 5.20 and 5.21.

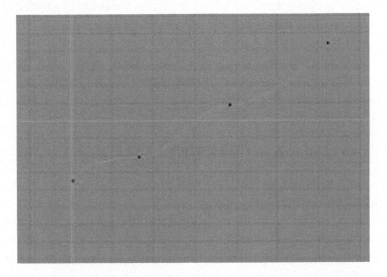

FIGURE 5.20   The motion curve of the car that went fast at first, but slammed on the brakes a few times to keep from losing control.

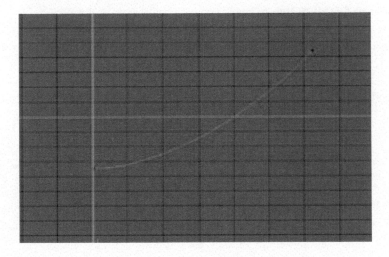

FIGURE 5.21   The motion curve of the car that steadily increased speed to the finish line.

Acceleration and deceleration is a natural part of organic kinetic motion. This is because of that rubber-band action we talked about in pose-based animation. The organic creature must wind up energy and then expend it, so the amount of that energy is not applied in a uniform manner, as it is with the robot. The kinetic energy accelerates to a point of maximum velocity (like our baseball pitcher when he releases the ball), then decelerates to rest. For this reason, we must create this effect in our animation or we run the risk of creating boring, lifeless, and robotic motion. The hallmark of good animators is their ability to create acceleration and deceleration in organic motion, and to know just where to use each. Without quality animation like this, there would have been no Disney, no Pixar, and no Saturday morning cartoons. This is a vital aspect of stylized and hand-keyed animation.

HOW DO I CREATE ACCELERATION AND DECELERATION?

Graph Curves and Tangents

In motion capture and rotoscoping, the sheer number of the keyframes creates the acceleration and deceleration naturally. Figure 5.22 illustrates a graph curve generated from motion capture. Notice how the rate of change is all over the place. When you capture a keyframe per frame of animation, the data is so dense that it will naturally reflect the motion of whatever was captured. There is no need to create acceleration and deceleration because it will mimic the film or video you are overlaying, which creates a natural acceleration model.

The one type of animation that does not have a natural flow of acceleration and deceleration is the pose-based animation, where we create

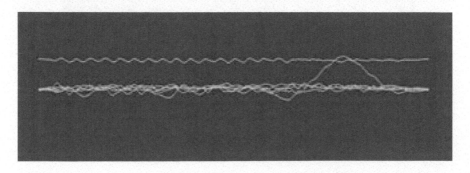

FIGURE 5.22   Motion capture data in the motion graph curve.

the keys for the main poses and let the computer do all the interpolation. This interpolation is the key element. It may be that our animation software is the apprentice animator, but that apprentice isn't very good! At least, he is a whiz at mathematical calculations, but he does not know the first thing about natural motion. Our apprentice animator can only divide the frames between A and B based on a mathematical equation. This equation is what we call a **tangent.** The tangent value tells him how to divide the interpolated frames and create the motion curve, which in turn determines exactly which value to put in at which frame of the animation. Remember, our animation software determines all of the values between keyframes. The tangent of the keyframe is what we use to sculpt those values to our content.

In order to understand keyframes and tangents, we first have to step backward a bit in time. Back to 1962, where a French engineer named Pierre Bézier first started using a universal curve system, now known as Bézier curves, in production at the Renault auto company. He was searching for a mathematical description of a curve, which would result in the exact same values no matter how big or small the drawing of that curve was, and he found several variations of algorithms to do so, implementing them in his auto body design work. That is a gross over-simplification of a very complex geometrical mathematical series of calculations, but don't forget that we are not here to do the math. We just want to know how it works and how we can use it. The point of this is that the curves, as they were then implemented afterward, were known as Bézier curves and they are used almost unilaterally in computer graphics to describe 2D and 3D curves. Bézier curves are used in a multitude of places, and we briefly discussed them in Chapter 3, where we went over NURBS curves and surfaces (Bézier is actually a different type of curve than NURBS). Here, however, we want to know about Bézier curves because they are almost unilaterally used in the creation of motion curves (sometimes called graph curves). Bézier curves consist of **handles,** also known as tangents, which is the mathematical term for the operation that determines the type of interpolation. Figure 5.23 is a motion graph curve from the Autodesk Maya software that illustrates the handles of the keyframes, which are the points on the graph, determine the rate of change from one to another. There is a tangent handle on either side of the keyframe, which shapes the curve as it goes toward the keyframe in time, and one that shapes the curve as it goes away from the keyframe in time.

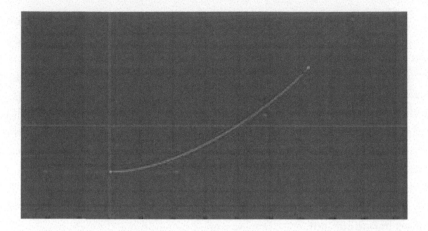

FIGURE 5.23 The points represent keyframes and the cross extending from them is the tangent handle. These can be edited to produce acceleration and deceleration.

The tangent handles of any keyframe can be edited in a multitude of ways, and they can be custom tailored to produce the exact change in rate of the value over time. However, there are several key automatic settings for the tangents that are commonly used in most animations. Remember that changing the tangent changes the rate at which the value changes over time. Following are several main types of tangents, with their associated nomenclature. Each software package has varying levels of tangent control, some more than others, but the following are the primary tools for creating and editing your animations in a life-like or heavily stylized manner. It is important to note that it is very difficult to demonstrate how an animation will look by using a still image. Once you are familiar enough with graph curves, you will start to be able to build an image model in your head of how the motion will feel by only looking at a Bézier curve, but for now you should experiment with your software of choice to get a better idea of what I am talking about. In the exercise material of this chapter, you will do a step-by-step animation that should teach you the basics.

Break/unify tangents—By default, tangents are unified, so changing the angle or weight value of the tangent will mirror the effect on the opposite tangent exactly. Breaking the tangents allows you to make the in and out tangent of each keyframe completely different, which

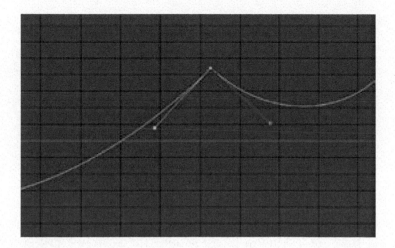

FIGURE 5.24 Broken tangents allow completely different in and out tangents from a keyframe.

makes it possible to have a different rate of change going in to the keyframe, and a different rate of change going out from the keyframe (which is often used in effects like bouncing). You can break or unify tangents at will on any keyframe (Figure 5.24).

Linear tangents—Linear tangents are actually not tangents. There is no curve at all, and the values change in a completely even way from one keyframe to another. This produces no acceleration or deceleration effect at all, which reads as very "robotic." When animating something with precise mechanical movement, linear tangents are often used (Figure 5.25).

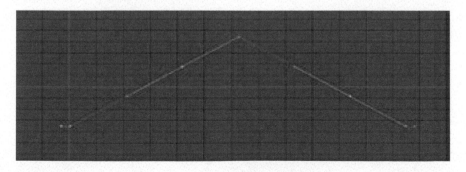

FIGURE 5.25 Example of linear tangents.

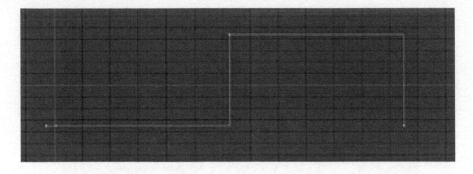

FIGURE 5.26   Stepped tangents.

Stepped tangents—Stepped tangents are not only lacking in tangent, but they are lacking in interpolation. The keyframe just switches values from one keyframe without any gradual change over time. Stepped values are great for things like visibility changes or teleportation, like whether it is visible, just "pops" on or off, or just materializes on the screen (Figure 5.26).

Smooth tangents—Smooth tangents change the selected tangent handle to be perpendicular to the normal of the animation curve, which usually results in completely smooth motion. It is smooth because the rate of change stays steady from one point to another, even through one keyframe to another. The rate of change stays the same not just from one keyframe to another, but throughout multiple keyframes (which is why it is often known as "smooth"). Figure 5.27 shows a simple smooth tangent on an animated motion graph curve. One important thing to note is that two keyframes with exactly the same

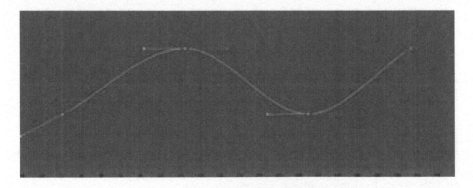

FIGURE 5.27   Example of smooth tangents at work.

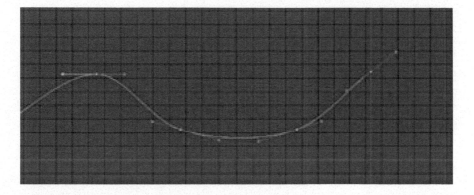

FIGURE 5.28   Example of the clamp problem, where the keyframes in the middle have the same value but the motion graph does not hold the value due to the tangents trying to evaluate smoothly between the keyframes, which will result in a "slip" of motion when playing back the animation.

value will not stay the same when interpolated as a smooth tangent. This means that if you have a car keyframed in one spot at frame 1, and the same spot in frame 10, the car will move when the animation is played, even though you have not keyframed any movement at all. This is the source of much head scratching and frustration with beginning animators because even though you have not created a movement for the object, it moves when you hit "play." The problem is in the math of the smooth tangent, which will not allow it to exit the keyframe as linear, or at least to retain the same value from one key to the next. You can see in Figure 5.28 how this problem occurs. The value *should* remain the same between the key at frame 1 and the key at frame 10, but if you played this animation, it would move as you see the motion curve indicating. The way to fix this is to change the out tangent to another type; in this case, linear or **flat** would work just fine.

Flat tangents—Flat tangents maintain a completely horizontal level in and out of each keyframe, which creates a natural acceleration and deceleration curve (sometimes these are called "ease in" and "ease out." In Figure 5.29 you can see the flat tangents and how they create a natural speed up and slow down change of rate between the values of keyframes. Flat tangents are better for organic motion because of this ease in and ease out. However, if over-used they become as boring and predictable (and therefore unrealistic) as linear tangents.

FIGURE 5.29 Flat tangents.

Tangent weights—In the more standard, non-weighted mode, the tangent handles have a fixed length, which makes only a certain combination of curve shapes possible between keyframes. Many times this is all that is required, and the default of most programs is to either not use tangent weights at all or have them disabled. Some software packages, however, allow you to make use of weighted tangents, which allows for far greater flexibility in tweaking and customizing your animations. Once tangent weighting is enabled, the tangent weights must be "freed" and you will be able to adjust the length of the tangent handles to create quite exaggerated motion curves, which are essential in creating certain effects like "hang-time" for objects that are jumping or thrown upward, or rapid acceleration curves (Figure 5.30).

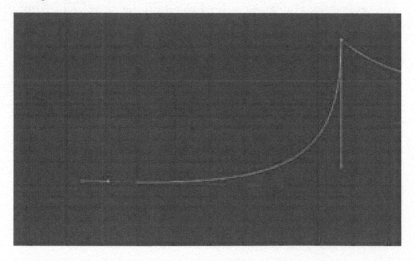

FIGURE 5.30 Weighted tangents allow extreme and custom acceleration and deceleration to occur without extra keyframes.

FIGURE 5.31   Acceleration curves.

Acceleration curves are created by tweaking the tangents to create an increased rate of change between one keyframe and another. Visually it looks like a steep upward or downward curve, which increases steepness as it reaches the next point. Figure 5.31 illustrates an upward acceleration curve and a downward acceleration curve, side by side. It is sometimes confusing to see acceleration curves as upward or downward because although the *rate* of change is increasing, the *value* the curve is moving from is not always increasing. An acceleration curve is generally placed between the rest and anticipation key poses, where the energy is being wound up, and the anticipation to the action poses, where the kinetic energy is being brought to its utmost velocity.

Deceleration curves are simply the inverse of acceleration curves—the rate of change decreases from one key to another, creating a "slow-down" effect. This is very useful for any action that has a kinetic absorption factor, like the follow-through pose we discussed earlier. Once the kinetic motion is expended, the body naturally comes back to rest and the energy is absorbed (Figure 5.32).

FIGURE 5.32   Deceleration curve.

HOW DO I BECOME A GOOD ANIMATOR?

Final Words about Animation

When stepping out on the road to becoming an animator, many people ask me this kind of question. How can I become a good animator? Should I go to school? What books should I read? What should I do? It is a very good question. First, traditional animation is an art form. 3D animation, at its core, is no different. The best animators are always artists, and many artists get into animation at an early age. However, if you are not artistically gifted or inclined and still want to be an animator, do not despair! Animation has many aspects, and being a good traditional artist is not always a prerequisite for doing good animation work. 3D animation is partially an art form, but it is also very technical. It must be technical, just because of the way it is done (on computers). So, the non-artistic animator might spend more time getting into character rigging or motion captures editing. Or the technical artist might spend his or her time working on procedural animation, which is based more on expressions and behavior scripting than pose-based keyframing. There are all kinds of places to excel in the field of animation. If you really love the idea of being an animator, however, you must spend a lot of time doing animation. People I have worked with in game development who were in the animation department spend hours animating every day. Whether they hand keyframed their animation or edited motion capture all day, they were immersed in it constantly. The problems that all animators face were dealt with so often, they had practiced solutions to them and those problems are universal in the world of 3D animation. I think that animation, more than modeling or rendering/lighting/materials, requires endless hours of experience in the practice of *doing*. It is a field that can only be truly evaluated in motion, and the ability to develop the eye to see art in motion as well as produce art in motion just takes time to develop. The one universal word of advice I give to aspiring animators is simply to constantly animate. Do not worry about modeling; do not worry about skinning, physics, cloth, fluids, or particle effects. Just concentrate on being the best animator you can be. If you animate a character made out of boxes but you animate it *well*, it will be more impressive than a half-done animation of a fully skinned character. You need to work on your ability to keyframe poses, create exaggerated motion, and edit your motion curves to produce eye-catching motion.

EXERCISE: THE BALL THAT BOUNCES ITSELF

In order to teach all the primary principles of classic keyframed animation, I have devised this simple exercise in Maya that goes over the following vital elements:

1. Setting keyframes

2. Squash and stretch

3. Pose-based animation

4. Acceleration and deceleration

We will be creating a "character" out of a simple sphere. This sphere will represent a squishy ball, which has the capacity for kinetic movement. We will create the illusion of a self-propelled character by using the elements of squash and stretch and exaggeration.

Step 1: Set up the Ball

First, create a polygon primitive sphere, and rotate 90 degrees in the X-axis so that the "pole" is facing the positive Z. Then enter pivot mode ("insert" on windows and "fn-left arrow" on Mac) and snap the pivot to the bottom-most vertex, using the point snap option (shortcut key "v"). Next, exit pivot mode and snap the entire object to the world origin, at the crosshairs of the grid as in Figure 5.33. This pivot placement allows us to

FIGURE 5.33 The pivot is at the lowest vertex and snapped to the world origin.

generate the squash and stretch from the contact with the ground, which will assist in the illusion of kinetic energy. Finally, choose Edit > Freeze Transforms in order to reset the local transforms to values of 0 in both rotate and translate channels, which will allow all subsequent keyframe values to start from this value.

Step 2: Setting the Key Poses

Now we are prepared to animate our ball. Remember those important key poses in our section on pose-based animation? We will be creating the illusion that this ball must generate its own kinetic energy by setting key poses of rest, anticipation, action, follow-through, and rest. Since this initial state is our first key pose of rest, we can set keyframes for the translate Y and scale X, Y, and Z channels. Select the channels in the Channel Box and right click, choosing "key selection." You will see the channels turn red, which means that they have been given animation data (Figure 5.34).

Next, scrub the time slider to frame 6 and set your anticipation pose. This will be your ball gathering kinetic energy, which is done in this case by squishing itself down into the ground. If the ball is made of elastic material, this will gather kinetic energy like pushing on an inflated ball. When you let go it will pop up off the ground. To accomplish this, we will set a keyframe at frame 6 with the scale Y at .5. Now, here we must maintain volume—the scale X and scale Z must also be keyed, but they must

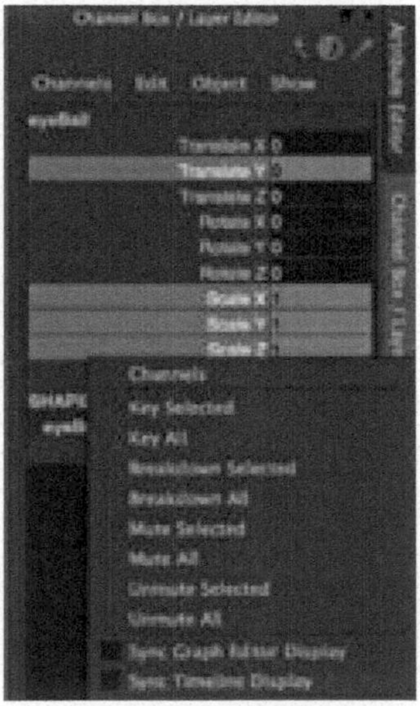

FIGURE 5.34   Key selected channels.

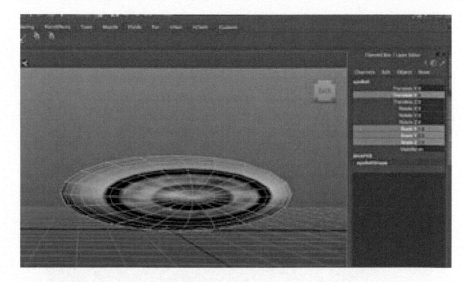

FIGURE 5.35 The anticipation pose. I gave our squishy ball an eyeball texture, just to be cool. Now he is short and fat.

be keyed at the inverse values of 1.5 for each. This is called squash and stretch. The basic formula I am using is as follows: scale.X and scale.Z = 1 + (1 − scale.Y). This is not the only squash and stretch formula out there, but it works well enough. Whatever scale you remove from Y you add to X and Z, and whatever scale you add to Y you take away from X and Z. This, combined with the pivot point being set to the ground contact of the sphere, will give the illusion that it is being squashed from its contact with the ground. Make sure you set keyframes at this pose (Figure 5.35).

The next pose is the action pose. What are we building all this kinetic energy for? So that we can jump off the ground. Go to frame 14 and set the translate Y to a value of 11. Since we have "popped" off the ground, we now need to stretch our squishy ball because like a rubber band, the energy has snapped and the ball has bounced off the ground. We want the scale of Y to be 1.5, which in scale terms is the opposite of a value of .5 because we have added value to 1 instead of subtracting it. Now do not forget our squash and stretch ratio. We want the scale X and scale Z to be set to .5 so that as our ball stretches longer, it also gets skinnier (Figure 5.36).

Now here, because we have a bounce, we have an extra rest pose. It is important to create this pose because we are dealing with physics and our squishy ball cannot really squish until it hits the ground. So, go to frame 20 and keyframe the exact same values as our original rest pose— translate Y is 0 and scale X, Y, and Z are all at a value of 1.

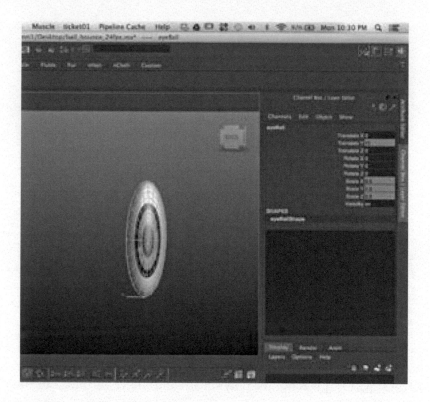

FIGURE 5.36 Actions. Our eyeball at full kinetic energy expenditure, bouncing upward and stretched all thin and svelte.

Our next goal is to create the follow-through. The follow-through for every kinetic action is a little different, but in this case, we have some physics to recreate, namely the act of our ball squishing as it hits the ground. The good news is that we can simply copy the same values from our anticipation pose to our follow-through here because it is essentially identical. Go to frame 24 and set the same values for scale X, Y, and Z (1.5 ,.5, and 1.5, respectively) as you did for the anticipation pose. See Figure 5.35 again for reference.

Now, finally, we can achieve rest pose once more as the ball springs back to its original shape. Go to frame 29 and set the rest pose as before— translate Y at a value of 0 and scale X, Y, and Z at a value of 1.

Congratulations! You have completed an animation. There is just one problem—why does it look so bad when you hit play? Good question. The problem is that while we have completed two out of three steps for animation—set key poses and tweaked timing (I cheated a little here and gave you the correct time for the keys)—we have not completed the all-important last step: creating acceleration and deceleration. Without editing tangents and tweaking the rate at which our ball squashes, stretches, and moves in the Y-axis, we cannot really make it a good animation. Right now, the motion looks flat and boring. We need to add the flair.

Step 3: Setting up Tangents for Editing

Open up the preset window configuration in Maya on the left-hand side of the interface, which has Perspective and graph editor, which will look like Figure 5.37.

We need to create a sense of acceleration and deceleration in order for our animation to have some kinetic energy along with our squishy ball— the rate of motion has to snap like a rubber band too. By default, Maya uses an "auto" key type, which sets the tangents of your curve mostly to be flat. This means that the in and out of each keyframe has an "ease-in" and "ease-out" curve that slows the rate of change from one point to another as it reaches the keyframe. This is great for mediocre, middle-of-the-road animation, but we need something a little snazzier if we want to make this animation pop (no pun intended). Your curves will look like Figure 5.38, where the tangents are all flat.

In order to get full access to our tangents, which will give us full control of the acceleration and deceleration, first we must set them up properly. Select the translate Y channel in the graph editor and select all the keyframes in the curve, which you can do by making a marquee selection of

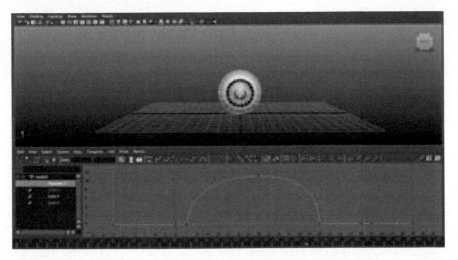

FIGURE 5.37 The bottom part of our interface is the graph editor, where all those tangents are accessible for editing.

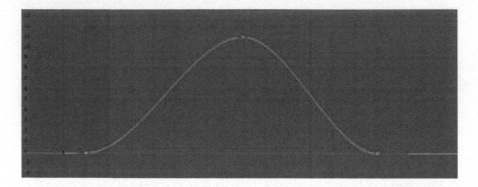

FIGURE 5.38   Flat tangents.

any part of the curve. Once all the keys are selected, you must first enable tangent weighting (which allows full control of the curves) by choosing the graph editor pull-down menu: Curves > Weighted Tangents. The tangent handles will have a filled circle appear on the end of each one, denoting that they are now "weighted." Once this is done, go to Tangents > Free Tangent Weight, which will free the weight to be edited. This will appear as an open square on the edge of each handle. The next thing you will do is break the tangents. This allows the in and out curve of each keyframe to be entirely separate. If we have them independent, we can be completely free to sculpt our motion as we see fit. This process must be followed for each motion curve that we want to edit properly.

What You Learned

- How to turn on weighted tangents

- How to free tangent weights

- How to break tangents

Step 4: Acceleration and Deceleration

The last and final step is to manipulate your tangents to create acceleration and deceleration. We will do this with our translate Y curve first, which is what controls the upward movement of our squishy ball. We need to create the illusion of physical forces affecting our ball, mainly gravity. For this reason, you will turn the curve into a "bell" shape by turning the outgoing tangents to be 90 degrees and shifting the weights of the handles of the middle keyframe outward until there is a sharp deceleration curve going into the keyframe at the top of the jump and a sharp acceleration

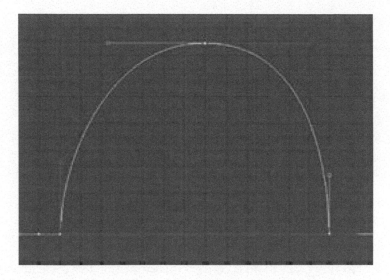

FIGURE 5.39   The proper "hang time" curve for upward Y movement.

curve going out of this keyframe. This will create the illusion of "hang time" or time when the force of gravity catches up with the upward kinetic force and starts to pull our ball back down toward the ground. Figure 5.39 shows you what this will look like in terms of a motion graph.

Are we done yet? Almost! The only thing you have left to do is to create the acceleration and deceleration action for the squash and stretch. There is a deceleration between rest and anticipation and a deceleration between anticipation and action. It is that rubber-band effect—it decreases velocity as it squashes and gathers energy, holds for a second, and then zzang! Explosive energy occurs, which slows down to a crawl before falling back to earth. Between the second rest post and the squash effect, you once again have an acceleration because the ball hits the ground and its squashing will "bounce" back to the rest pose. Therefore, between the follow-through pose and the final rest pose you have acceleration because the kinetic energy will be harder to gather as it squashes, and then snaps back as it stretches into the final rest pose. Figure 5.40 illustrates the proper squash and stretch curve of the scale, which you can follow along with the video tutorial.

What You Learned

- Creating acceleration and deceleration

- Simulating the force of gravity with motion curves

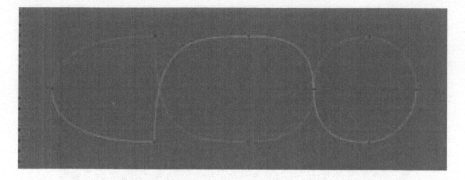

FIGURE 5.40   The scale X, Y, and Z curve showing the inverse relationship of the scale values to maintain volume using squash and stretch.

Step 5: Generating Cycles

The very last thing we will do is convert this animation to a cycle. It will be short, I promise! The great thing about the cycle is that we already have it. We just have to shift our time a little in order to see it. The cycle we can create, without generating a single keyframe, is to shift our range slider to start at frame 6 and end at frame 23 (omitting the last frame will prevent a hiccup from occurring when the first and last frame of the animation are the same). Now when you play the animation on a loop, you will see that it constantly plays repeatedly, as if the squishy ball were bouncing contentedly forever.

In order to do this within any range length of animation, we can simply choose a method of infinity. Infinity allows us to cycle or offset an animation forever after the last keyframe. In order to set up the style of infinity, you must choose Curves > Post Infinity > Cycle (or other option) and the curve will repeat itself indefinitely throughout the animation. You might need to tweak it a bit to get the curves to match up properly (Figure 5.41).

And that's it! You have completed your exercise-based guide to core animation skills in Maya.

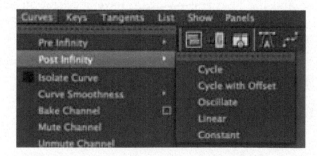

FIGURE 5.41   Infinity settings.

CHAPTER 6

Conclusion

Y OU MADE IT! This is the final part of the book, where we wrap up everything we have learned and give some sage advice to young, aspiring 3D artists. I assume now you must be an accomplished modeler, rendering guru, and animation master, right?

If only it were that easy. My point here, at the end of the book, is that you will have become none of those things by reading through this book and doing the contained exercises. You should, however, have a very solid foundational and conceptual knowledge of how basic 3D graphics work, and how to approach certain tasks with certain tools in any 3D software package. Modeling, rendering, and animation are the three key disciplines in 3D graphics, and now you know the important aspects of each and how to go about reasonably creating content. Many aspiring 3D artists ask me questions about what they should do and how they should go about getting a job or furthering their knowledge in 3D art, and I always have the same advice. Find out what you are good at, and specialize in that. Not many people out there are good at modeling, lighting, material editing, UV texturing, and animation. People have specific skills in specific areas (or at least a pressing interest), and when they pursue that aspect over others they often excel more in it. You do need to learn how everything works, though, which is the purpose of this book. If you do not know anything about geometry you can never be a good texture artist, and if you do not know animation you will not be able to model properly because you will not see the object or character in motion—you will always see it as a static model. When you know how everything works, you become much better at your special area of expertise. So pick an area in which you would like to specialize and focus on taking your learning in that direction. There is so much room to learn, grow, and even innovate in the broader field of computer graphics that you can pursue one aspect of it for a decade and not really scratch the surface. I have been working with 3D graphics in one capacity or another since 1996, and there are aspects of it I have never used at all. It is a big field, and narrowing down what you really want to do early is a great way to get good at it without clogging up your brain with aspects that are not that important, like cloth simulation, facial animation, fluid effects, or subsurface scattering. The three cornerstones of 3D, however, are modeling, rendering, and animation, as described in this book, and if you have these under your belt as foundational knowledge, then I am sure you can learn the rest when and if the time comes. Good luck on your path to becoming a great 3D artist!

Index

FIGURE 2.5   Minnow Pete, modeled by the author.

FIGURE 2.6   A lower polygon, triangulated version of Minnow Pete.

FIGURE 2.58   Original, low-poly models by author.

FIGURE 2.59 Same models after smoothing. The angular edges are gone, but the polygon count has almost tripled! Always strive to use the least polygons possible when modeling.

FIGURE 4.3 Real-time rendering of a game in development by the author.

FIGURE 4.4 Software rendering. Notice the high quality of this render. It could never be achieved at 60 frames per second (fps) with today's hardware.

FIGURE 4.24   The effects of using colored lights are very noticeable. Use it sparingly.

FIGURE 4.37   The sphere on the left has a specular or "shiny" shader, while the sphere on the right has a non-specular shader.

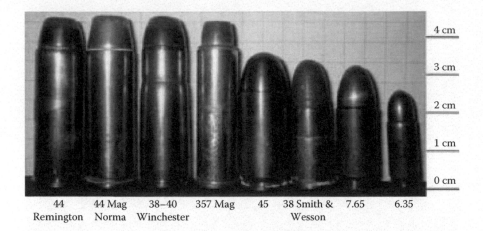

| 44 Remington | 44 Mag Norma | 38–40 Winchester | 357 Mag | 45 | 38 Smith & Wesson | 7.65 | 6.35 |

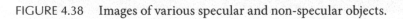

FIGURE 4.38 Images of various specular and non-specular objects.

FIGURE 4.39 Lambert shaders do not have specularity.

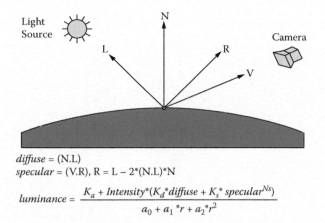

diffuse = (N.L)
specular = (V.R), R = L – 2*(N.L)*N

$$luminance = \frac{K_a + Intensity*(K_d*diffuse + K_s* specular^{Ns})}{a_0 + a_1*r + a_2*r^2}$$

FIGURE 4.40 Calculations for specularity on a Phong shader.

FIGURE 4.41 The cosine power is higher on the right and lower on the left.

FIGURE 4.42 The sphere on the left looks more like gold, while the sphere on the right looks more like plastic. This is due to the difference in the specular color.

FIGURE 4.43 Blinn shaders have more sophisticated specular controls.

FIGURE 4.44   The ball on the left is using Anisotropic shading.

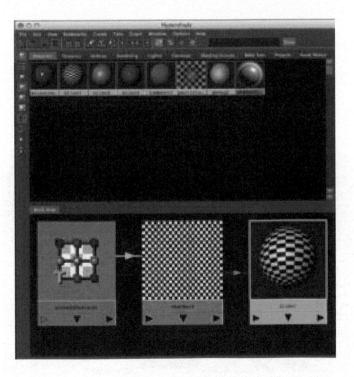

FIGURE 4.45   The material editor in Maya (called the Hypershade). Often the materials are called shading *networks* because the information is stored in various *nodes*, which are then connected together to form a network.

FIGURE 4.46 The ambient color value on the right sphere is turned up, which multiplies the value of the diffuse color after the lighting is calculated, which is why this sphere is red.

FIGURE 4.47 Incandescence multiplies the value on top of the entire rendered sphere, making all of the pixels brighter at once.

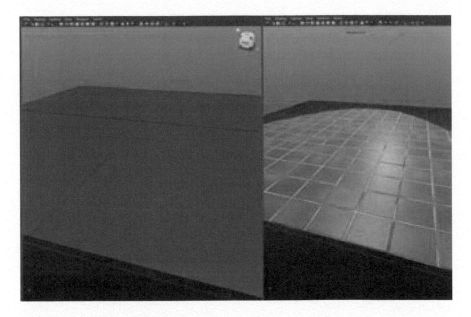

FIGURE 4.48 Notice that the illusion of "texture" or dimples and grooves is created without heavy geometry. This is done using a bump map.

FIGURE 4.49 Illustration of a dirt map in use.

FIGURE 4.50 The sphere on the right has no translucency while the sphere on the left does.

FIGURE 4.51 The translucency focus has been increased to allow the light penetration to fall off over the surface.

FIGURE 4.52   The sphere on the left has a reflection value of .3, while the sphere on the right has a reflectivity value of 1.

FIGURE 4.53   An area has been defined telling the reflection where to be, and where not to be, using an alpha value to put a white square on a black background, white denoting a full reflective value and black denoting no reflectivity.

FIGURE 4.54   The sky texture is placed as a reflection color on the sphere on the right, which "fakes" the reflection instead of using ray tracing to generate it.

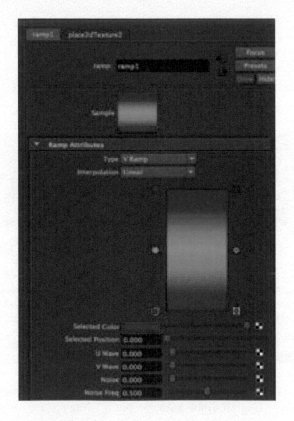

FIGURE 4.55   A ramp texture in Maya.

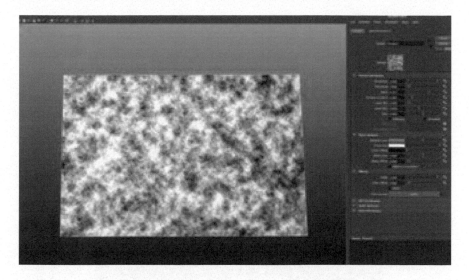

FIGURE 4.56   A fractal texture with it applied to a polygon plane on the left.

FIGURE 4.57   The rendered orange with skin textures.

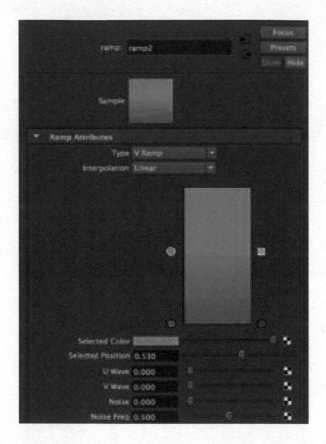

FIGURE 4.58 A ramp was used to generate a soft gradient from darker orange to lighter orange.

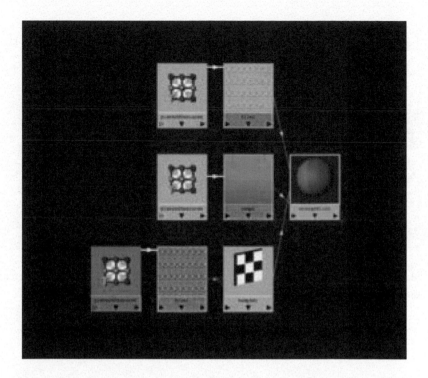

FIGURE 4.61 A snapshot of the shading network as it appears in Maya. This is why they call it a network. It is many nodes for just one material.

FIGURE 4.64 The left side is the UV editor view, which displays the 2D texture image and the faces as they relate to it. The right-side view is the 3D view, where the pixels of the image are re-rendered on the 3D object as mapped out in the UV editor.

FIGURE 4.65 The 2D image of the can is wrapped around the cylindrical projection.

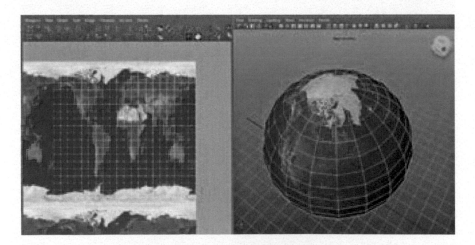

FIGURE 4.66 The "saw-tooth" UV coordinates allow each triangle to have its own set of UV points, making the spread even on this texture.

FIGURE 4.67　The pinched UV coordinates at the poles of a sphere create only a single UV point for all the triangles at the poles, which result in warped texture coordinates.

FIGURE 4.68　An unobscured view of the saw-tooth UVs from Figure 4.66.

FIGURE 4.69   An unobscured view of the pinched pole UVs from Figure 4.67.

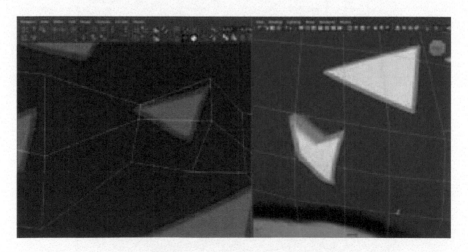

FIGURE 4.70   The poor UV layout on the left results in distortion and streaking on the right.

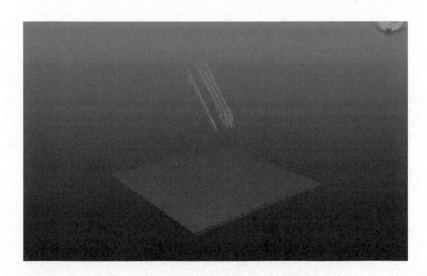

FIGURE 4.71   Poly plane and directional light at an angle.

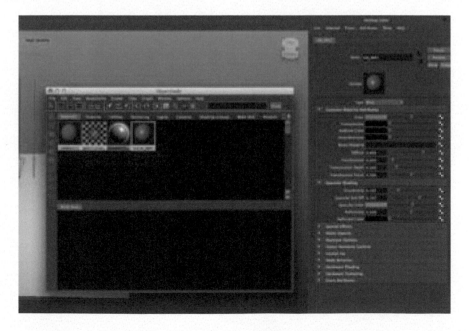

FIGURE 4.72   Hypershade and attribute editor open in Maya.

FIGURE 4.73   Creating the file texture.

FIGURE 4.74   Color tile texture map.

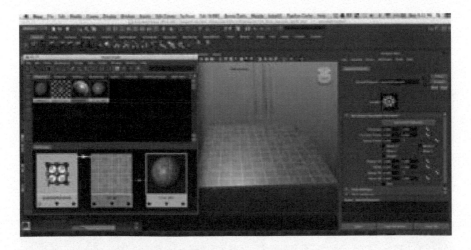

FIGURE 4.75   Repeating color tile texture on object.

FIGURE 4.77   Look how much detail we can get with a bump texture map. It looks like a much more complex piece of geometry.

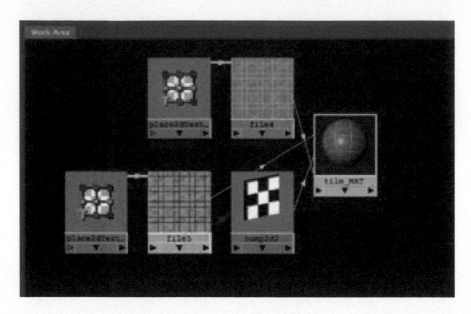

FIGURE 4.78 The completed shading material network.

FIGURE 4.79 The completed real-time render. The specular map is subtle but makes a big difference.

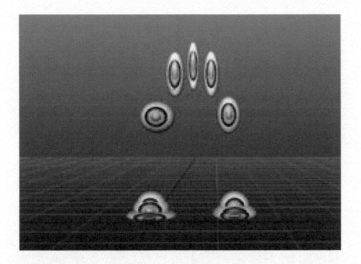

FIGURE 5.1   Bouncing ball animation with ghosting.

FIGURE 5.2   Ghosted character animation.

FIGURE 5.6 A character rigged with joints that are animated by rotation. (Character design and model by Bert Farache, rig and skeleton by author.)

FIGURE 5.7 Early cell drawings of cartoon characters would be done in "key poses" or important breaks in movement. The apprentice would frantically sketch in all the "tween poses." (Courtesy of artist, Topher Putnam.)